# India Rising

## But Who Will Make It Happen?

# India Rising
## But Who Will Make It Happen?

J.N. Rampal

PEACOCK BOOKS

Published by
PEACOCK BOOKS
7/22, Ansari Road, Darya Ganj,
New Delhi-110002
Phones : +91-11-40775252, 23273880, 23275880, 23280451
Fax : +91-11-23285873
Web : www.atlanticbooks.com
E-mail : orders@atlanticbooks.com

Branch Office
5, Nallathambi Street, Wallajah Road,
Chennai-600002
Phones : +91-44-64611085, 32413319
E-mail : chennai@atlanticbooks.com

*Peacock Books is an imprint of*
*Atlantic Publishers and Distributors (P) Ltd*



Printed in India at Nice Printing Press, A-33/3A, Site-IV,
Industrial Area, Sahibabad, Ghaziabad, U.P.

# Preface

It has been really exciting times for India and Indians lately. In every forum and in media, everyone is gushing about India's rising stature these years. The India everywhere at Davos in 2006 and five years thereafter, the welcome to the high echelons in international affairs, the new adjectives appended to her achievements in industrial development and some very nice figures in various economic projections, gladden every Indian heart. For instance, International Monetary Fund's *World Economic Outlook* (*WEO*) Database (April 2011 Edition) states that Indian economy will grow from US$ 1.54 trillion to US$ 2.78 trillion by 2016. John Humphry of 'Institute of Development Studies' puts year 2050 size of Indian economy at US$ 27 trillion. An optimistic Citi Bank study puts the figure at US$ 85 trillion on PPP basis.

So very nice! I am wondering whether my happy mental state is an irrational exuberance rather than sensible elation. Because one of my dear friends, who has been an angel investor in many a high tech ventures, would say about projections, "next quarter is short term, next year is long term, and rest is astrology". Also, in the other corner of mind is a nagging apprehension that won't go away, and the thought is that India has many times been crowned the 'highest potential' nation, but sooner or later, the promise fizzles out because of one reason or the other.

To add to this, the economic projections come with the usual economist's riders. The pre-requisites that are often mentioned are that (i) India must improve its governance and regulatory framework, (ii) build institutions for finance, education and research, and (iii) scale its infrastructure by an order. With all these pre-requisites together, the projections about India dominating the world economy in future can mean anything.

To add to conflict of ideas in my mind, another event presented itself in late 2011. Suddenly, the Indian rupee became weak against foreign currencies (Rupee dropping from 44 to 55 for a dollar in Nov-Dec 2011). Why sudden flight of investment, if the Indian economy has as much promise as being bandied about by so many organizations and experts?

So what is happening? Are we getting there on the top of the world, or is it merely a pipe dream? Or is it somewhere in-between? The catch-22 (dilemma) has been visiting my mind so very often. There have been numerous occasions when I thought, "Oh let me sit down and give the issue a serious treatment". And finally I did. This is how this book came into being.

Having done many sector-wise projections for my consultancy organization, for ascertaining the market potential in aviation, defence, infrastructure and homeland security, I found that the long-term prognosis after liberalization has always been positive for India. But the figures in recent projections have had a mesmerizing effect on me. So, I set about putting together a new, bullish brief on 'The India Story' for the organizations that were spawning new initiatives in the mentioned domains. After consultations with peers and a little research, soon I was in the middle of a maze of information in the form of projections, reports, causal analysis, Ministry and Planning Commission websites and many other Internet resources. I also found some very informative and detailed studies and analysis papers published by international investment houses, 'think-tanks' and consulting organizations that gave thumbs up to achievement potential in a wide variety of domains within the Indian economy.

Then the difficulties started. Firstly, the many data-sets that I accessed from official or commercial resources had dissimilar frames of reference. Some provided data on year-on-year (YoY) basis, while others average decadal (10 year steps) data. Some stated the figures in US$ values in real terms with a particular year (e.g. 1990 or 2000) as base, whereas some data was on purchasing power parity (PPP) basis. So assuming that absolutely correct information was provided by all these sources (which is obviously an impossibility), I was still left looking at a variety of values for the same chunk of information.

If a non-expert sifts through all this information, there is yet another problem. The information is not as per her/his reference frame of knowledge. Understanding an economist's excel sheets or World Economic Forum's declarations may not be the best way to get a good feel of the state of India's progress or future potential for a layman.

But why would we need an average Indian to know about the state of India's economy or the projections for the future? This question is not rhetorical. Maybe all the intended audience for this book has this question (like they say) 'on the tip of their tongue'.

An expert may assume a dismissive, schoolmasterly tone and say, "because it is required". But I guess this question deserves serious contemplation and a cogent but 'easy to understand' response. Firstly, all of us Indians need to know the possibilities that our children face in emerging India and prepare them for earning and leading a good life in the evolving environment. And secondly, the mulling and contemplating possibilities on this question can give us a deeper understanding of issues involved and enable us to enhance our collective contribution for the India's rise.

My effort to understand the possibilities and issues did give me a much better view of present scenario and 'envelop' of the future, and in addition, laid the foundation of this book.

So let us try to get a good answer to this question. Let us begin with our supposition (and everyone's projections), that India is at the threshold of a momentous rise, economically, politically and by many other measures that you may choose from. But this is only a bright possibility. India has some great advantages at this moment in history, but converting this potential into real achievements will require a very large number of stakeholders (millions of Indians in multiple roles) to strive together. Before millions of Indians put their efforts together, they would need to be aware of the range of the possibilities and their plausible contribution to this mighty endeavor and of course, they will need to acquire the required knowledge, skills and tools to be a part of this great expedition. Expecting millions to have a consultant's analytical skills to find this out by themselves is a non-starter, so we need to provide a panoramic view of the India Story to the people at large and give them a starting point for their exploration. The book is a humble effort in that direction.

During the writing of this book, there have been many instances when conflicting thoughts in my mind reached a deadlock, with no resolution in sight. It is worth sharing some concepts that helped me to untangle the Brownian motion of competing perspectives. A few words on these concepts may help making the context more readable.

The first concept that came very handy is that of fuzzy logic. One is sometimes forced to take a position in digital mode. You have to choose between this or that, 0 or 1; true or false. But most organic things vary in a continuum, or are multi-valued but not linear (continuous). Take the example of effectiveness of a regulation or organization. You can't say they are totally ineffective or have perfect efficacy. So there can be a linear scale (a set of equidistant values like 1, 2, 3, 4, 5) or a fuzzy set (a set of irregular values like 5, 11, 12, 56, 78) and the measure may be one of these values. The concept comes in handy when we want to capture the status of composite and complex variables like business environment, competitiveness, etc. In Chapter 4, we use 'Dashboard'—a pictorial representation of important composite variables, whose conglomeration indicates the status of India's progress at various vantage points in time. For simplicity, we provide five levels for value indication. These five levels are not 1/2/3/4/5 (or 20%, 40%, 60%, 80% and 100%), but the five fuzzy logic values for each variable, e.g. for corruption the five values are (1 Rare, 2 Isolated, 3 Scattered, 4 Widespread, 5 Everywhere), or possible GDP of India in 2050 (1 US$ 40 trillion, 2 US$ 50 trillion, 3 US$ 56 trillion, 4 US$ 77 trillion, 5 US$ 88 trillion). The interaction of fuzzy entities (aggregation, multiplication, ratio, etc.) is a little more complicated than normal algebra, but that is of no consequence to the topic at hand. We use fuzzy representation for a better understanding of various factors and leave the complexity of fuzzy maths for later.

The second concept that has found repeated application in this text is that of 'Gaussian distribution' (also called normal distribution), which quite aptly describes aggregate characteristics of many communities and collections. According to this concept, the collection following this distribution has a distinct mean (called mu) and a continuous bell-shaped spread around it.

An example for normal distribution could be the height of children, say in class 7. We expect these 12 year olds (or a few months younger or older) to be about 152 cms in height. On the average, we will find that for a school class, 68% will be in 152 ± 5 cms height range, 95% within 152 ± 10 cms range and 99.7% within 152 ± 15 cms range.

Without getting into technicalities, we could say that 152 cms is the mean height and 5 cms is variation (called sigma in technical terms). And in the expected 'normal distribution', 'one sigma' measure of variance dispersal contains 68% of population, 'two sigma' 95% and 'three sigma' 99.7%. It is useful to apply the distribution to all human clusters, e.g. voters, workers, buyers, etc. Each collection will have its own mean and own variance. For example, engineering students' IQ will have a higher mean than factory workers' IQ. Weight of population has a lower mean in Thailand than in US. Similarly, variance is different for different clusters, e.g. temperature variance is more in deserts than in coastal areas. So whenever we are talking about characteristics of a class, we are looking at various combinations of mean and variance.

Our motivation in using the concept of normal distribution is that it encapsulates the behavior of composite parameters like policies, quality of education, infrastructure, etc. quite well.

The philosophical opposite of this concept is generalization, where we paint all members of a class with the same brush (like inheritance of all parameters in object-oriented programming in software). Generalization could be our worst enemy in objective discussions. For example, we may generalize that all politicians are corrupt, all Indians are good at IT, all US scientists are bright, all Boeing aircraft are safe, etc. Objectively, all goodness consists in having a higher goodness as mean and lesser variance, and politicians' corrupt image is the result of honesty mean being low and lesser number of them being under the curve where honesty varies between 80% and 100%.

The crux is that it is never 'black' or 'white' but one of the grays in-between. It is a matter of proportions and all human endeavors are to get the proportions right.

A word about a concept called 'tragedy of commons' used in our reasoning later. It is a term popularized by Garrett Hardin in an article on Science in 1968, in which it was argued that when people share a common resource, those who take the most, gain the most. But everybody suffers the consequence of the resource's decline equally. Overexploitation of groundwater in India and cutting of forests by mafias are classic examples. In the context of issues under discussion, many cases will appear in our later discussions. For example, the fruits of democracy have disproportionately found their way to select groups, and the legal recourse is badly configured to target the poor for minor transgressions, while the powerful get away with murder (literally). 'Tragedy of commons' is the most apt description of hijack of India's democracy by its entrenched elite and the nouveau (newly) rich.

Another useful concept that helped analyses and inferences is the Pareto principle, also known as the principle of factor sparcity, the law of vital few or simply 80-20 rule. This principle indicates that 80% of essence value is generated by 20% of the population. That points towards unequal value contribution by factors. Conversely, 80% of the problems could be created by trouble spots which are 20% of the population. This principle allows our analysis to focus on factors with heavier weightage rather than enumerating all possibilities. Brevity would not be possible otherwise.

A 'statutory warning' for the purists is in order here. The information and the data sets used in this book are more indicative than 'verifiable' model-based calculations. The idea is to convey the 'sense of the issue' (the fun in using the word 'sense' has been taken away recently by the Indian parliament, when they passed a 'sense of the house' in supporting the 'Lokpal bill' in all its majestic form one day, and then started punching holes in it immediately afterwards). Let us stick to the old conventional meaning, i.e. we pursue the sifted/averaged/ gist information as a tool for understanding the direction in which things are going rather than as values which are sort of 'contractually guaranteed'.

It is my earnest hope that the book encourages awareness, understanding and participation in the 'India Emerging' journey. If it can trigger objective thinking in the minds of young Indians about India in 2020 and beyond, my effort would have succeeded.

**J.N. Rampal**

# Contents

# Contents

# 1

# Cycles of Change

## Introduction

Before we start deliberating on India's ascent in the coming future, let us try to familiarize ourselves with some thoughts from history on how human experience has gone through cycles of change. We may also get some indications about how nations have grown to greatness in the earlier passage of history; and look for those pointers in case of India's progress.

A philosophical thought first, attributed to Clarence Manion, Dean of Notre Dame Law School,

> Man begins his existence in bondage, and rises,
> from bondage through spiritual faith,
> from spiritual faith to courage,
> from courage to liberty,
> from liberty to abundance,
> from abundance to selfishness,
> from selfishness to complacency,
> from complacency to apathy,
> from apathy to dependency,
> from dependency back into bondage.

The sophists will call it the natural sinusoidal lifecycle of all things organic, the theologian will call it the human failing that keeps them from becoming God.

But human beings do follow the rise and fall of a sinusoidal curve, pure or distorted.

Does the same kind of 'cyclical life' principle apply to aggregate humans, to cities, to nations or to civilizations? Are the nations and civilizations doomed to alternate between rise and fall, from Zenith to Nadir on a regular basis? Is it dependent on human intellect only or do other factor ease or exacerbate this up/down seesaw? Living in the scientific world, let us abjure Voodoo (let go of the philosophical and theological aspect), and look at the causative and measurable factor for hints.

For the purpose, let us retrospect some historians' thoughts about the process of evolution of human race. Many have hypothesized on how humans progress from one level of sophistication to another over the centuries and ages. For the sake of brevity, we examine two streams of thought for patterns that could help us to ascertain the plausible causes and then help us project the possible scenarios of the future.

We are looking for clues about how unraveling of new technologies, change of cultural and political environment affects the progress of the societies, nations or the world as a whole.

### A Peep into Evolution of Human Experience

The first such school of thought (worldhistorysite.com, 2005) propounds that the world progresses from one civilization to the next, when discovery of *new technology* extends the human capabilities and better *means of communications* spread the progress to a larger population. The process also spawns new forms of institutions and social mores.

To trace it in the known history,

> The discovery of writing (earliest examples being the Egyptian picture-like hieroglyphics) in the third century was the first known instance of communicating through writing. The prowess came about as 'hunter-gatherers' transformed to agricultural society and coalesced further to four great empires—Roman in Europe, Parthian in Persia, Kushan in India, and Han in China.
>
> The alphabetic writing soon followed, though the practice was restricted to the educated elite for many centuries. The philosophical thought and religious practice was a reserved domain for the elite and it gave us feudal and aristocratic societies. Generally it was the King who ruled the lives of subjects helped by a loyal

retinue of philosophers, religious leaders and military generals. The laity did get a whiff of knowledge, even if it was only to cement their position as the faithful followers of the throne and Church (or equivalent religious authority).

The real spread of knowledge was made possible by commercial printing press in the fifteenth century and can be considered the beginning of creation of literature, art and exploration of science. Society now became organized in nation states. The better informed subjects now got a say in the governance of nations and democratic form of government took root in most nations (communism was just another form of peoples' participation but assumed dictatorial hue along the line).

Twentieth century saw the culture of mass media take center stage. Electronic technologies such as the television, radio, cinema and telephone became the communication media. Culture and science became universally diffused and global competition created a frenetic pace in scientific, cultural and military advancement by nation states. The move towards inter-mixing of societies and multi-level synergistic trade became an unstoppable wave.

Twenty-first century has seen the ubiquity of the electronic communication, email first and internet now. The universal availability and usage of internet (and all the knowledge base associated with it) has democratized the world like nothing before. By allowing man to machine communication, the expanse of information available to individuals has increased by such astronomical proportions that it makes earlier forms of information devices (books or videos, etc.) look redundant. The world is now a global village; with dependencies between nations and societies so entrenched that industrial activities (and even wars) cannot take place without the help of many others.

Thus we see that technology and communication has defined a new level of advancement for human race each time these have undergone a quantum improvement; and have also brought about a change in political and social institutions. We are seeing the beginning of yet another quantum leap with the advent of wideband communication and cyberspace. We don't yet know how it is going to pan out in 20 or 50 years. But this is one of the major enablers for India's rise, as we see in later discussions.

The second 'culture evolution' (evolutionaryeconomics. wordpress.com, 2012) concept traces a correspondence between new weapons discovery and extinction of civilizations in a simple decametric 720 + 72 years cycle (Memetic cycles). Copper arrows and shields, Bronze spades and chariots, Iron Armour, Cavalry and Gunpowder have been the evolution steps in this parade of greater efficacy of weapons. The warriors, who had access to later generation weapons, have prevailed upon the adversaries with older generation weapons. Nuclear weapons have been the game changers in the last fifty years, but their supremacy does not seem to be lasting the 800 years as suggested by the Memetic cycles. Information is the latest weapon that may cut short the reign of nuclear weapons very soon.

Motivated by these two well researched evolution models, let us make do with a simplified composite schema of evolution, which will suffice for the purpose of having a generic view of flow of human civilizations. The human race has through four broad stages, namely,

1. Earliest recorded agriculture-based society (Mesopotamia 3100 BC, Indus 2500 BC, Aegean 2000 BC, China 1600 BC, and Americas 1200 BC, Mediterranean 1000 BC). Served by crude individual weapons and means of communications. Limited to local fiefdoms and scattered human civilizations with rare contact with other cultures.
2. Regional civilizations (AD 400-1500) Greek, Rome, China, Persia, India. Expanding influence, empire building. Philosophical thought and religious fervor

still under control of select elite. Power projection through massive armies with iron swords. Contact with other cultures through explorers and enterprising travelers.

3. Global civilizations (sixteenth to twentieth century) colonies, empires, polarized world. Marked by increased dissemination of knowledge by printed material, and later by evolving electronic means. Journey towards a mutually conversant and dependent world begins. So does the quest for control. Rise of world powers, which hold disproportionate control over other nations. Military might now consists of multi-dimensional (air, land, water, underwater, and lately space) dimensions and highly effective explosive weapons. Last two decades of twentieth century saw democratization of knowledge, flattening of economic, military and political power hierarchy of nations. And enormous increase in trade and other contacts between different cultures and nations.
4. A Global village. The twenty-first century redefining the political and economic equations. The technology and knowledge widely disseminated and internalized. Industrial and military superiority now more fleeting and province of the willing and persevering. Industry and trade are now globally networked. *The Second Coming of the EAST*.... The journey has just begun.

## Recent Global History

Let us now have a look at the recent history of human civilizations in slightly finer detail to ascertain the changing equation between the nation states. The global civilization (sixteenth century onwards) started when the Indian and Chinese civilizations were at their zenith and Europe was just embarking upon the 'Industrial revolution'. The quest for markets and raw materials provided the basic push for sea-faring and imperialism and we saw the ascent of industrial societies in Europe and later America. Indian and Chinese civilizations had peaked and their decline gave the European industrial nations the space to exercise their new found techno-industrial might. Soon the world was divided as 'areas of influence' between the European powers, England, France, Portugal, Spain, Belgium and Netherlands.

The two world wars in twentieth century can be seen as a hidden manifestation of competition between various industrial nations for control over global assets and geographies. An unintended consequence of Second World War was the rise of two superpowers, i.e. United States and USSR. The competition between these two, now lodged in history books by the name Cold War created a bipolar world, in which most nations aligned with one of the two. The military pacts and trading blocks created two major flows of human progress. The technology, which became a differentiating competitive advantage, became a precious asset to be developed and guarded jealously. And then the boon of 'Information technology' arrived.

Till then, the computation technology was the preserve of a select few. The apex of technology was United States, closely followed by UK and other European countries, and a desperately 'trying to catch up' USSR, who after mastering the vacuum tube technology, were way behind in semiconductors. Internet, which started as a project in US 'Department of Defense', changed the way the whole world looked at information. Now, the proliferating internet allowed the whole world to open to a wide expanse of knowledge. The veil of secrecy over technology was lifted. Information technology flattened the competitive field by enabling laggards to absorb and use technology quickly for their progress. Not for nothing this epoch in history is being labeled "The Information Age". Consequently, the rise of East Asian tigers and many other smaller nations like Singapore and Taiwan further distributed industrial progress in a decentralized world.

If the last 20 years of twentieth century brought a cataclysmic shift in the distribution of knowledge and industrial prowess of various nations, the process seems to be only accelerating in the twenty-first century. There are many reasons that it is happening, though the starting pulse was provided by the mentioned IT technology enabling wide dissemination of knowledge. The labor arbitrage and demographic shifts has necessitated the transfer of work and therefore spread the fruits of the progress to an even larger part of the world.

The cultural cycle also has a considerable part to play in this. Yet another unintended consequence of the Second World War was the demise of classical imperialism (colonizing by European powers). After exploitation as a source of raw materials for centuries, the newly independent nations tried to achieve all-round progress by diversifying into industries. These nations adopted varying models and schemas for development, but by and large, these nations moved away from being exploited as a source of raw materials and/or a ready market for Western goods. These erstwhile captive entities transformed to either a synergistic partnership or brought them in direct competition with Western economies.

To sum up

1. We are at the cusp of a tectonic shift in the world. The leadership positions in global economy and diplomatic power are being shuffled like a pack of cards.
2. The change is being driven by 'Information Technology' and specifically the internet revolution. It is pertinent to mention that 'Google' and similar tools have increased the knowledge diffusion beyond measure.
3. The stages of the cycle of civilization 'Ascent, Peaking and Decline' are being seen to be at 'changeover' points, Western countries beginning to decline; and India, China and others beginning their ascent.

   There are many more; others in BRICS category and Indonesia, who will complete the picture of this shift. But the main theme still remains the same, i.e. 'Decline of the West and rise of the East'.

An additional factor that does not reveal itself clearly from our retrospect of human history, is the demographic shift. We will explore this aspect in detail in the following section.

## Evidence of the Shift

Now that the world is at an inflexion point, we seek to identify the major dimensions along which this changeover is revealing itself. We also look at the snapshots at various vantage points to understand the direction and magnitude of this change.

Amongst the emerging countries, China is ahead in economic matters, while India has a lead in establishing institutions and administrative regime. Similarly there may be other parameters, which may help us understand the relative strengths of the new powers with respect to each other and relative to the declining powers. But building the snapshots by focusing on four parameters paints a clear view of changing positions. Two of these parameters, i.e. military and economy are traditionally called hard parameters, because the superiority in these can be used coercively. Culture is called a soft parameter, because it is used more for inducing rather than forcing. Demography is a parameter that happens due to a multitude of reasons and is not classified as either hard or soft (but has the same effect as a hard one).

So let us see the shift along these parameters one by one,

### 1. Economy

For discerning the shift in economic strengths of various nations, a study published by PricewaterhouseCoopers in March 2006 provides clear pointers. The chart below shows the comparison of two blocks of nations. G7, in this study, comprises of the advance economies, i.e. US, Japan, Germany, UK, France, Italy and Canada + Spain, Australia and South Korea. E7 comprises BRIC + Indonesia, Mexico and Turkey.

There have been follow up studies by Pricewaterhouse Coopers, IMF and many other consultancy organizations on the topic. Some may have different scope or focus but each and every of these studies confirm the sense of the visual below. The later studies also indicate that the E7 nations are accelerating even more.

(Light colour bars relate to G7 and dark colour to E7)

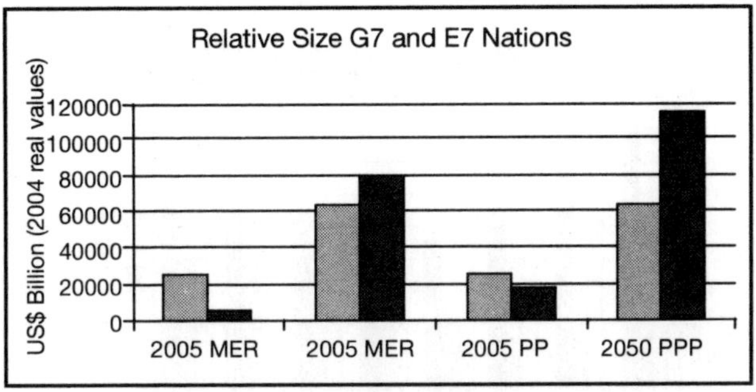


*Source*: PricewaterhouseCoopers Report "World in 2050", March 2006

[*Note:* The graph is presented 'as it is', but the second set of bars from the left relates to 2050 MER and not 2005 MER as written.]

This visual hides an enormity. Though in real terms the size of G7+ economies was more than 7 times the aggregate of E7+, in Purchase Power Parity, it almost equalizes. But in 2050, when real value between the two groups is US$ 80 trillion and US$ 62 trillion, the PPP places E7+ way ahead. And more recent studies are now showing that E7+ is going to be ahead even on real value dollars.

(*PPP measures the actual local value of money. If a hair cut in New York costs US$ 5 and in Delhi, INR 25, then in case of haircut, US$ = INR 5. If we take a basket of everyday needs and calculate equivalence in similar manner, the average value of currency equivalence can be computed. This is Purchase Power Parity.*)

After 2008 financial meltdown in US and the recent European Sovereign Debt crisis, the shift has only accelerated. Further updates of projections by PricewaterhouseCoopers (http://www.pwc.com/en_GX/gx/world-2050/pdf/world-in-2050-jan-2011.pdf) and other organizations confirm this.

Looking at it another way, by comparing contribution of the two groups to global growth, we can clearly figure out who is going to be more energetic in economic activities in the coming future. This informative chart from 'HSBC global

Research' provides a clear view of slow but consistent shift underway.

**Contribution in Global Growth**

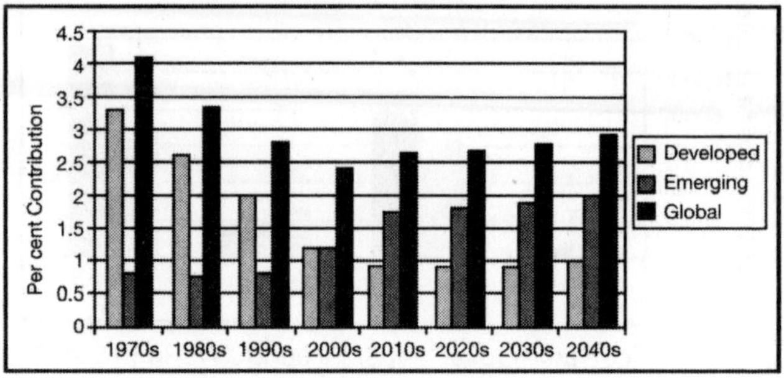


*Source:* HSBC Global Research: The World in 2050, January 2011

Look at the left most of three bars (western world contribution) going down and white bars (overall global growth) getting dragged down along with. It is only after 2000 that the magenta bars (emerging economies) start steadily increasing their contribution and pull up the global growth (white bars) thereafter.

The contribution in global growth has been rather asymmetric till 2000, the Western economies contributing a lion's share. But because of repeated financial meltdowns in the developed nations, their economic growth has stalled. On the other hand buoyant emerging nations start increasing their contribution, and in 2000 the two groups are seen to be contributing equally. But in this process the overall global growth has slowed down from >4 per cent in 1970s to 2.4 per cent in 2000. The emerging economies have begun making a larger contribution (quite possibly double the proportion as compared to Western countries by 2050) to drive the global growth upwards once again. The global growth rate is expected to rise above 3 per cent by 2050.

To summarize, the size of the emerging economies is catching up with that of the Western economies. Their rate of growth is also accelerating and overtaking the Western world. The economic weight of nations is clearly shifting from the Western world to emerging nations.

Out of these nations, China and India have disproportionate leverage because of many factors. To mention the most important, their population size (and hence size of the market and also available human resources for industrial progress), and educational/cultural lineage. We will have quite a bit more to discuss on that later.

The other emerging countries (Brazil, Russia, South Africa and Indonesia) and the continent of Africa have not been given sufficient coverage in our treatment as yet. These countries will have their own leverage to affect the global economy as per their capacities and size. The aggregate effect is not insignificant, but with a focus on India, we will leave detailing of their contribution for some other time. Similarly Africa may be the 'magical continent' after 2025, because they are just about waking up from the long slumber of servitude to imperialism, and fratricidal civil wars. With the abundant natural resources that Africa is endowed with (minerals, oil, forests and people), if they put their house in order, there is no reason why African nations will not become a power to reckon with in a few decades. Even their demography will be magical in fifteen years from now (lot of young people entering working age population, when other populations are aging).

In gist, we have very clear signs of the cyclic change of economic prowess taking place in front of us. Sometimes we tend to see only micro events and not the macro flow. So a lot of press about sub-prime mortgages, deficit reduction, downgrading of sovereign rating by Moodys, impending Greek default, structural adjustment by other south European nations (Italy, Greece and Spain), slowdown and cutbacks in UK, danger to French banks, bailouts by European Central Bank and IMF, and so many events that we read about or hear, are nothing but manifestations of the shift in economic power from the Western countries to emerging countries.

### 2. Demography

Unlike any other times of substantial change in human history, there is one phenomenon that is happening for the first time. Earlier generations have seen only one kind of demographic change, i.e. increase in population. The rate of increase has waxed and waned according as a consequence of wars, epidemics and natural calamities, but the population, and by derivation the number of young people have always increased in all cultures and societies. There might have been large migrations too, but increase was still the norm. That has changed in recent times.

The population of the sparsely occupied world reached 1 billion in the middle of nineteenth century, and was 1.4 billion at the beginning of twentieth century. It doubled to 3 billion in 60 years and the earth's surface started looking nicely occupied with nation states filling up all the areas marked by boundaries (except the polar regions, which now are the target of frenetic race for occupation and exploitation). By now, the politicians and economists had started talking about the perils of over-population. The population growth was unbridled in poor countries or countries with cultures/religions that considered family planning a taboo. The alarmist politicians/economist (generally in the Western world) started talking about scenarios where the civilized world (read Western countries) will be overrun by the uncivilized hordes from uncivilized societies. China and India always had a special mention in these reports as the possible source of such scourge.

The world population doubled again in the next forty years to 6 billion in 1999 and recently, we celebrated the arrival of 7 billionth child in November 2011. But the tune and tenor of the discussions about population and demography has taken a curious turn.

What has happened meanwhile is a consequence of something called prosperity. Call it nature's revenge, or cyclical twist of fate, the peace and prosperity have brought in a modus vivendi and mores in the global society that threaten the very existence of the same peace and prosperity. The prosperous societies have become more individualistic, the occupations have turned more stressful, people have less time (and inclination) for family and marriages and children are not seen as assets but liabilities and bother.

The contemporary world has enjoyed the longest period of peace (cold war and other regional wars notwithstanding) and economic growth (despite greed induced financial roller coasters and political upheavals). That has changed the lifestyle and work-life in advanced countries in a way that the fertility rates have been going south. In addition, with better medical care and dietary discipline, the life expectancy has increased. So suddenly we have a distorted demographic pyramid. Rather than having a lot of young children and enough people in working age group of 19-59 years, we have more gray haired population. In the Western world, the pyramid is so lop-sided that these countries don't have enough people who will create value, but more who need support, whether government provided or individually managed. There are many ways to understand the transition from one demographic snapshot to another, but we can look at two of them to get the feel of the matter.

The first is the provider/dependent ratio that is calculated by dividing working age population by the support dependent population. A word about the denominator (support dependent population), it now contains less children (who will sometime transition into working age population) and more senior citizens (who will not). This ratio is likely to go down from 2.15 (2010) to 1.4 (2050) in Europe, as per a study by Commission on Growth and Development, Study paper no. 32.

The second indicator of the demographic shift is the median age, as per a paper published by Center for Strategic and International Studies; "Graying of the Great Powers", March 2008. Median age is a figure, which is the middle of the age spread of a nation. Half of that nation's population is below the median age and the other half is above that figure. Until the beginning of twentieth century, no nation had her median age greater than 30 years. As recently as 1950, the highest figure was 36. By 2008, 8 of the 16 nations in Western Europe had a median age higher than 40. By 2050, 6 will have a median age >50. In conjunction with the fact that 18 countries today (44 in 2050) have contracting populations, the prognosis looks even darker.

We should make an *important differentiation* between a demographic forecast and other forecasts. The demographic forecast has comparatively a very high certainty. All people we are making forecast about being 50 years old in 2050 are already 10 years old in 2010. Unless a meteor hits earth, or the doomsday prophesies of one of the eccentrics comes true, these people are going to be there proving the projections. Fertility and death rates are also monitored in real-time for other reasons (census, social security, marketing, etc.), so the accuracy of these projections is also likely to be close to certainty (for the purist, it tends to the probability of 1 asymptotically). Consequently, we are really seeing unprecedented and sweeping demographic changes with strategic, economic, social and political consequences.

There are many repercussion of reducing birth rates in the Western world and now the whole discussion has shifted from the earlier "Invasion by the uncivilized hordes" to carefully managing the migration of skilled aliens to keep the economy floating in Western countries. Many countries are already below replacement rate levels, i.e. despite long lives, more people are dying than are born each year, so the total population is decreasing.

The demographic shift phenomenon has challenges for India and China too. China has reaped the benefit of a young population till recently. But in a measure to control 'population explosion' in 1960s, the 'One Child' policy put sudden brakes on population growth. This has created an artificial crevice in the flanks of the population pyramid. In 2020, when the 1960 generation retires, the aging process will catch up with China too. And in 2029, Chinese population will start shrinking because of the twin effect of 'One Child' and prosperity. This will happen, when China is still short of 'advance nation' category (per capita income basis). How China handles it will be keenly watched, and will perhaps will throw a lesson or two for India too, which is going to be in similar situation by 2050.

India has not been able to institute coercive policies for population control. So the reduction in birth rate has been because of voluntary adherence to 'Birth Control' and recently because of increasing prosperity of the middle class. The dent in the side of pyramid is not significant therefore. The lack of effectiveness of 'Family Planning' program has become a blessing in disguise.

However, the population numbers in themselves are not sufficient to ensure the growth of a nation. The large numbers of prospective workers need significant effort in creating enablers like education and training, and amenities like urban housing and transportation. China has pro-actively scaled up these enablers, but India's stance has been 'one step forward and two steps back' on these issues. It is a big challenge for India to invest in these enablers to take advantage of this momentary (On the time scale of history, 40 years is just a fleeting moment) demographic advantage. If not, all these millions of prospective workers could become problem children remonstrating and demonstrating on the streets.

To conclude, the demographic advantage has shifted from the Western world to emerging economies. But let us underline the qualifying edict, that the advantage has a 'use by' date. The unique advantage will last China another 15 years, India 40 years and Africa a little longer. If you don't seize the opportunity and encash it by then, it is gone.

### 3. Military

Military power is perhaps the clearest (and scariest) manifestation of a nation's, King's or individual's power. Looked at from a sovereign's or leaders' viewpoint, he/she has an obligation to use the military prowess in the interests of the nation or group whenever and wherever the other options have been exhausted. However, there is always a lurking desire to use it because the military option will always seem to be the quickest, easiest and most effective option. The only down side is that military power is expensive. So you can start brandishing your sword only if you have loads of Dollars or Gold or any other universally acceptable currency for buying that shining sword, and a nice scabbard too.

By this logic, it also follows that military power projection is possible only if the economy is booming. If the economy gets into decline, it is not very long that one can keep firing guns on the strength of dollars that you do not have.

Just by the way, there is also an 'oft believed' assumption that nations/groups are ruled by informed individuals with high intellect and welfare on their minds. But this assumption is as good as 'Rational Markets' assumption in the study of economy and have shown similar consequences in history as the rational market hypothesis recently demonstrated.

In more than many instances in history, the rulers haven't been the most cerebral people. Some, in addition, had the predisposition to support their pre-meditated preferences by application of military might. Sometimes the wars were triggered by the megalomania or sheer arrogance of such leaders.

It may be an exaggeration to compare display of military might by such rulers with another human idiosyncrasy called 'game', which is a clear display of manhood (with a gun of course) against wild animals. I carry a very vivid impression of 'Shikar' (Animal hunt) from the times of Maharajas in Indian history, wherein a kill was a show of the royals' might against powerful wild animals like tigers and lions (sometimes rhinos as well), and the defeated animal, after being shot (sometimes by the minions), was reduced to a trophy to be photographed with.

The decapitated heads, mounted torsos and stuffed bodies would then be the symbols of power to be used in drawing rooms as adornments.

Sometimes, the animals were skinned so that their fur could be used as rugs in the sitting room.

From a tiger's viewpoint (if anybody bothered to think about it), however, this was the ultimate subjugation to naked power of the gun.

One really wonders whether the megalomaniac humans are averse to delivering the same 'tiger' treatment to other humans or nations. Without getting into too much of recent history, maybe some have detected a hint of similar feel in the treatment of axis powers at Potsdam Conference. Many other recent wars can also be put into perspective with the 'tiger' logic. It is either grabbing resources when you can't have them by trade negotiations, or grabbing power, when you cannot get elected, or neo-imperialistic alignment of nations to a particular political system. Life isn't fair. Wars are even less so.

There are some other facets of the military power projection. Military strategy is, (1) an extension of the political philosophy of a nation, and (2) draws sustenance from the economic strength of that nation. As indicated earlier, as shift in economic power gets underway, the military strategy also follows afoot.

In the recent history, the superpowers and associated military groupings have waged many wars with many a justifications, but the underlying policies have been enunciated 'tongue in cheek' to be one or many of the following:

1. Political influence extension.
2. Making the other military grouping lose war.
3. Extension of boundaries into neighbors' lands.
4. Ethnic conflicts.
5. Control of oil reserves and pipelines.
6. Acquiring and Securing transportation routes (land, sea lanes).
7. Annexation of markets.
8. Rare earth resources.
9. Winnable wars (the low hanging fruit).

The wars however, are always couched and packaged in moralistic terms, for example,

1. Fight for democratic principles.
2. Fight against evil empire.
3. Fight against imperialism.
4. Fight for human rights.
5. Fight for making world a safe place.

It is no coincidence that the military adventurism is the exclusive domain of the economically powerful. They are the ones who can afford it. After Second World War, most wars were waged on consortium method by Western powers or Warsaw Pact countries (Communist block). There have been some others, who have run their own private wars for control over minerals and natural resources in Africa. But that was possible only if the economically powerful were absent from the scene.

This schema of military strategy and projection has continued after the Second World War. However change has been noticeable recently. It has been noticed in four forms:

1. Cutback on military expenditure. Examples abound, but the most discussed on electronic media are, (a) Massive reduction in Russia military and space programs, (b) Decommissioning of UK carrier fleet, (c) Closure of US bomber and advance fighter programs and many other programs in other countries. In fact, military industrial complex of advance nations is in decline, their business is reported to be down by more than 40 per cent in 2010. "It's been a great ride," said Rockwell Collins Inc Chief Executive Clay Jones at a conference hosted by Credit Suisse and Aviation Week. "But the ride's over." (*Reuters*, 01 December, 2011)
2. Retreat from the current engagements earlier than the military commanders thinks feasible and desirable. Afghanistan is one battlefield wherefrom Soviet Union withdrew earlier and Western forces will withdraw soon. Similarly withdrawal from the gulf has been quick and as some feel, before the Iraqi democracy has established itself. Military pacts are fast becoming non-functional. Gone are the days of CEATO, CENTO, and Warsaw Pact. NATO also is seeing reluctant participation by many member countries.
3. Preference for diplomatic engagement rather than confrontation despite provocations. (At a level that would have induced a military response in earlier times.) No saber rattling with a newly aggressive China.
4. Technology denial policy giving way to collaboration. For the Indian market, there is fierce competition for selling military hardware, nuclear power plants, even materials/systems, which were earlier denied due to proliferation concerns.
5. China's military build up causing changed security perception in APAC.

This shift in military strategy clearly indicates a shift in economic power from Western world to emerging nations. Even with technology excellence, the Western powers and Russia are willing to reverse the earlier policy of denial to the new economic powers.

### 4. Cultural Evidence

The following is quiet an amazing fable and I am sure anyone born in the twenty-first century will refuse to believe it. And because it is anecdotal, no claim is made about the veracity of the story.

It goes like this.

> After the Second World War, all nations faced the reconstruction and economic growth challenges, some more than others. So preferential trade and (helping each other with) aid (especially by Western countries) became the norm. South Africa was still an apartheid country, so their cooperation was limited to only 'white' countries. (It is OK to poke fun at apartheid, as everyone officially hates apartheid.)

Soon Japan became quickly industrialized, especially because US and UK lent a particularly bounteous helping hand. So in 1970s, South Africa determined that Japanese were also white and it is OK to do business with them.

As they say, some more water flowed in the Ganges and in 1980s, Chinese were also granted 'White' status by South African apartheid regime.

Well, there is more than jest in this anecdote. The cultural preferences, likings and disliking change with power equations, more specifically with economic power changes. In the tumultuous Indian democracy, don't we see the local shopkeeper catapulted to 'Sahib' status soon after winning the municipal elections? If it is true for individuals, it must be true for many as well. Nations treat the other ones with respect if they are powerful, especially economically powerful.

We have seen that effect in recent times. The emerging nations are not talked down to anymore in the world forums.

Rather than have the standard harangue of not maintaining human rights, and workplace standards, not controlling population, not protecting IPRs, etc., the dialogue is more about trade barriers, balance of trade, currency exchange rate controls.

In fact, there is a larger role to play for emerging economies in international forums like World Bank and IMF and talk of recasting Security Council in United Nations. In fact the recent European Debt crisis has seen participation of emerging economies in finding a solution, and more importantly, the emerging economies are being asked to don the mantle of donors. Talk of reversal of roles?

With this, the cultural stereotypes have also been shed and new ones adopted. Chinese, once shown as same color drab uniform wearing, semi-skilled factory workers in decrepit factories are now considered to be the most cost conscious, efficient manufactures in the world. Indians, once considered too busy with their spice laden, multi-regional, smelly food, are now considered the most competitive and hardworking knowledge workers and are blamed for taking away even the American jobs because they are willing to deliver equivalent value at lesser cost. The Taiwanese, Singaporeans, Koreans, Brazilians, and a long list of nationalities have come out of a sub-par list to rub shoulders with the best in the world.

The US president's usual refrain about Chinese and Indian students outdoing the US children is the new acceptance of intellectual equivalence of the emerging nations. The students from emerging countries outscoring others, is no more a surprising event in US universities. The ascendance of emerging countries in other activities like sports, arts, entertainment and leisure only confirms the fact that emerging countries are becoming equal in cultural matters too.

Thus, the cultural acceptance of the emerging nations also points to the fact that emerging economies are now on ascendance in a world that is seeing the developed countries to accept their equivalence at least, if not their niche superiority.

## Conclusion

We are at the onset of a monumental shift in the world affairs. The world is now transiting into a fifth civilization cycle based on ubiquitous information revolution and resurgence of the East, specially India and China. We see the patterns of change whenever the new technology and better means of communications (basically the platforms for knowledge dissemination) develop. Those who harness these have an 'early bird' advantage in the race for progress.

There are clear indications under way as seen by the relative shift in crucial parameters of economy, military power, demography and cultural prowess between various nations and groups.

The East is on the rise again and India and China are on way to assume the leadership positions in the world.

That is the prognosis. But is it a given, a fait accompli? Can we just relax till it happens as a matter of time, quite like the proverbial lazy man under the date palm waiting for the ripe dates to fall straight in his mouth.

More specifically, is India assured of her rise to the second largest economy (or perhaps top slot as predicted by Citigroup) in 2050? Are there any conditions or challenges? Are there any indicators that will tell us whether it is going the right way? We examine these issues next.

# 2

# A Brief History of India

India is a melting pot of civilizations, races, cultures, religions, in a way that no other place in the world is. For centuries, the Indian subcontinent has seen flowering of civilizations, their plunder by numerous invaders from land and sea, given shelter to many who were forced out of their native lands and stayed on, and has allowed intermixing of beliefs, faiths and races. The diversity of people is equally matched by diversity of her landscape. India extends from the icy Himalayas in the north to the warm vastness of the Indian Ocean in the south; and from the marshlands of Kutchh and desert of Rajasthan eastward towards the evergreen forests of Assam and eastern states (seven of these states called 'Seven Sisters' for their environmental similarity). The culture is an amalgamation of many sub-cultures that have developed independently over many millennia. They say if you want to experience all the weathers, colors and creeds of the world on one Visa, Go to India.

The current culture is a resultant of many centuries of seeding, growth, destruction, metamorphosis and synthesis of religions, philosophies, cultures and social mores. Let us look briefly at how it happened.

## Glimpses of the Past

### *The Early Civilizations*

Called the "oldest living civilization of earth", the Indian tradition dates back to 8,000 BC and has a continuous recorded history since the time of the Vedas, believed variously to be 3,000 to over 5,500 years old. Many early civilizations spawned and prospered on the river banks and coastal areas and then spread inwards. The Indus Valley Civilization, which flourished in the northwestern India from 3300 to 1300 BC, was the first major civilization in India, with manifestation of its sophisticated and technologically advanced urban culture at Harappa. This Bronze Age civilization was followed by the Iron Age Vedic civilizations, which extended over much of the Indo-Gangetic Plains. In one of these kingdoms, Magadha, Mahavira and Gautam Buddha were born in the sixth or fifth century BC and propagated Jain and Buddhist philosophies that have become widely practiced religions of the world today.

[*Source:* History of India From Wikipedia, en.wikipedia.org/wiki/History_of_India]

Almost the entire subcontinent was conquered by the Maurya Empire during the fourth and third centuries BC. It subsequently became fragmented, with various parts ruled by numerous middle kingdoms for the next 1,500 years. This is known as the classical period of Indian history, during which India has sometimes been estimated to have had the largest economy of the ancient and medieval world. According to economic historian Angus Maddison in his book *Contours of the World Economy, 1-2030 AD: Essays in Macro-economic History,* India had the world's largest economy during the years 1 AD and 1000 AD controlling between one fourth and one third of the world's wealth. That opulence is supposed to have continued up to the eighteenth century.

Much of northern and central India was once again united in the fourth century under the Gupta Empire, and remained so for two centuries thereafter. This period, witnessing a Hindu religious and intellectual resurgence, is known among its admirers as the "Golden Age of India". During the same time, and for several centuries afterwards, southern India, under the rule of the Chalukyas, Cholas and others experienced their own golden age.

### The Mughals

Muslim rule in the subcontinent began when the Arab General Muhammad Bin Qasim conquered Sindh and Multan (in southern Panjab of the modern day Pakistan), setting the stage for several successive invasions from Central Asia between the tenth and fifteenth centuries. Babur, a Turkish-Mongol adventurer and distant relative of Timurlane and Genghis Khan, established the Mughal Dynasty, which lasted for 200 years.

Mughal rule covered most of the northern parts of the subcontinent. Mughals introduced Central Asian art and architecture to India. Indian courtly culture evolved into a unique blend of Hindu and Muslim traditions. In addition, in other parts of the continent, several independent Hindu states, such as the Rajputs, Vijaynagar Empire, the Marathas, flourished contemporaneously. The Mughal Empire's gradual decline in the early eighteenth century, allowed the British gain ascendancy over South Asia.

### *The British Rule*

Beginning in the mid-eighteenth century and over the next century, large areas of India were gradually annexed by the British East India Company. Subsequent to the Indian mutiny (called first war of Independence by us Indians), India was directly administered by the British Crown and witnessed a period of both rapid development of infrastructure and economic decline. Considered a captive source of raw materials and market for British goods, the Indian industry died out. From the zenith of being largest economy of the world in seventeenth/eighteenth century (Angus Maddison, 2007), India was reduced to the low of penury by the time British left brutalized India. The situation was made starker by a mismanaged partition at the time of independence, which caused perhaps the worst bloodletting in the contemporary history. Millions were targeted in the 'free for all' mayhem by goons and zealots all over the subcontinent. The hastened and therefore lop-sided bifurcation of infrastructure left India holding some pieces of rail, roads, military, and logistics apparatus. Pakistan faired no better and had to immediately start seeking international help.

### *The Bloody Partition*

More than fourteen million refugees, half of them relocating from India to Pakistan; and similar numbers in the other direction, made a journey across the newly carved out India-Pakistan borders to their new homelands. Hindus, Sikhs and

Jews moved to India and Muslims westwards to Pakistan. But the vitiated political and ethnic environment was soon to cause eruption of paranoia and violence at a scale that was unprecedented.

Most tried to take trains (even on the bogey tops). However, even an early exit was no salvation. My father told me a story of the times as follows:

> One trainload of Hindu refugees arrived at Amritsar from Lahore, but there were only blood splattered bodies, all massacred in the train itself. There was also a chilling message written in blood, on one of the train bogeys that said, Isko kahte hain katai (this is called cutting). That is when the madness took over at Amritsar. A similar orgy of death took place on the train going to Lahore with a macabre counter message 'Isko Kahte hain safai'. (This is what is called cleaning up.)

Those who could not make it by train, tried to take whatever means of transport available to them. Bullock carts were available but no good for a fast carriage. Others, who could not even put up a bullock cart just tried to leg it across the border. These caravans also faced the armed crowds on the way and either fought their way out or perished.

Some, who waited for the governments to do the needful for a peaceful passage to their new homelands, were left at the mercy of killer mobs and the result was streets littered with dead bodies at the mercy of vultures and dogs.

In all more than half a million perished. Some put the figure at more than a million. Just to understand the scale of the mayhem, 3 per cent of the Indian population was massacred in their own homeland, thanks to the shortsightedness of the British Crown and the politicians of the day.

In addition to the burnt landscapes and 15 million displaced persons, it left such mental scars that a few generations have lived with the hallucinations of being chased by marauding mobs all their lives, in addition to losing all the material possessions, lands and many family members. It is only now that new generations born in India cannot visualize those monstrosities, the pain and anger have gone out of the collective memory of the society.

Just to mention the contrasting scenario across the border, where the partition is still kept alive by politicians and religious bigots for petty gains, even the new generations continue to suffer the trauma vicariously long after the train loads of refugees, the big tented refugee camps and the burnt out villages are banished into the history books. The whole world has got on their feet and gone on, but some keep on twisting the knife for letting the pain linger.

### *Getting Up and Getting On*

After the blood stopped flowing, there was a crying need to rehabilitate the refugees. On the Indian side, special camps were built for receiving the people coming over, and with alacrity, the government moved in to rehabilitate these people, who had no assets except their skills and courage. Free allocation of land was a big help for these displaced people to start over their lives again. Kingsway Camp in Delhi and Panipat, an industrial town north of Delhi became the magnet for attracting people who had business skills. It goes to the credit of these hardy people, that within 25 years after partition, most of them were indistinguishable from those who were already living in India. Most had joined the burgeoning successful businessman community of North India. Their entrepreneurship (perhaps driven by the will to succeed in dire circumstances) has certainly raised the bar for small and medium businesses, especially in trading and mechanical engineering.

### The rebuilding of Economy

Let us now switch back to our discussion on economic growth of Indian subcontinent after the independence and partition. From the high of more than a quarter of global GDP in the mid eighteenth century, India had come down to less than 1 per cent of global economy by the time British departed. The country needing to rehabilitate millions, building industrial base, building institutions of governance faced an uphill task.

In addition, with the end of Second World War and start of cold war, there were many push and pull factor that faced the new leadership of India.

Luckily the Indian leadership, drawn from the Congress party, that had spearheaded the freedom struggle under the stewardship of Jawaharlal Nehru and with intellectual guidance of Mahatma Gandhi, set out to build a self reliant India. India got the fundamental things right. The framework of a secular, democratic republic with a written constitution that provided equality and basic rights was the harbinger of long term good for the people of India. There were many challenges, internal and external, but the collective will of people exercised through a democratic process always propelled India on the path of progress.

Not that there were no hiccups. Right in the beginning, Pakistan, that had been carved out of India as a peaceful homeland for Muslims, decided to live by its hatred of her earlier mother ship, i.e. India. The war to annex the valley of Kashmir started right after partition.

Though pushed back and largely defeated in 1948, the Kashmir annexation dream is always kept smoldering by successive Pakistan rulers, military or civilian, by foisting wars and skirmishes across Indian borders. Wars in 1965 and 1971 have been followed by many mini-wars, and the situation even now remains tense. Enmity between the two countries remains a high-cost standoff, more for Pakistan, but it still bleeds India. The other neighbor China punctured the 'bonhomie' between the two countries (the successors of two great ancient civilizations) with a border attack in 1962. Thereafter, by constant diplomatic needling, China has never allowed the mistrust to die. The Western countries have never embraced India because of her perceived tilt towards socialism (and by inference, Soviet Union) during cold war. The democratic build up has been marred by sectarian violence, corruption and terrorism.

Because of the external and internal reasons enumerated above, the velocity of the progress has been stunted, but the direction has always been right. The self sustaining democratic rule and the correction mechanisms (elections and institutions) have obviated big deviations from the path many times.

### The Era of Change

The slow growth after independence can be seen as a consequence of socialistic policies, and also because of the baggage of inherited problems. The population growth was another factor that would annul modest gains made by agriculture and low tech manufacturing (we were making cycles and mopeds more than cars and airplanes). On the expenditure side, defense required increasing allocations because of inimical neighbors. All in all, Indian economy was struck at a 3 to 3.5 per cent growth rate. This rate of growth was so characteristic of India, that the economists dubbed it as "Hindu rate of growth". There were other adjectives too. While the east Asian nations were termed 'Tigers' because their nimble footed policies for growth; and China as the 'Dragon', India was likened to an 'Elephant', a large creature unable to run.

A big departure, from the slow and arduous 'Hindu rate of growth' was ushered in 1980s by the then government headed by Rajiv Gandhi. Manmohan Singh, as a finance minister was given the responsibility to shape the new economic policies to usher in quick growth. In part, the policy push was also triggered by the looming 'balance of payment' crisis in mid-1980's. Thereafter, succeeding governments, whether forged by one political party or the other, have sustained this economic policy direction. India has been able to maintain sustained high growth (more than 8 per cent) for two decades and that has put India in the big league. In fact, China sees India as the only real competitor ahead in the global scenario, be it economic, military or political prowess.

As in 2010, India stands at an epoch. India has a large economy, growth of which is driven more by internal consumption than by exports. The economic fundamentals are right. The financial system is democratized and reasonably efficient, the industrial base is well diversified (though not best in class in many areas except knowledge services), and the educational system is deficient but scaling and developing. The regulatory environment is the 'Achilles heel' and needs serious effort to become enabling rather than a 'millstone around the neck'. But the biggest advantage that will decidedly tilt the balance in the favor of India is her upcoming demographic advantage.

We will drill a little deeper to understand the current Indian capability in these dimensions one by one in this chapter.

## The State of Indian Economy

"Sarv Jan Hitay, Sarv Jan Sukhay", i.e. universal benefit and happiness for all citizens. With this as a basic tenet, India made a choice to adopt a 'socialistic pattern of society', a phrase attributed to Jawaharlal Nehru. The unintended suggestion of the proclamation was that the India intended to adopt Soviet model of central planning, emphasis on heavy industry, focus on employment generation (even by under employment) and preference for self-reliance (rather than coordinated approach with friendly nations in various political or industrial groupings). The education and research being at nil to nascent level, the approach was doomed to failure or at most deliver paltry results. It was more of idealistic naivety rather than hard nosed real politic. So, for three (lost) decades, India was stuck with a few victories and a 'Hindu rate of growth' (less than 3.5 per cent per annum), while many peers galloped away. Plentiful of examples exist, none of them very charitable for the policy makers. One such glaring case is that of the car industry. Japan and India started car industry at about the same time (early 1950s). Even the car they built was the same model, Morris Minor, for which UK provided technical know how. Japanese car companies Toyota, Honda, Mitsubishi and many others, had become world beaters by 1980; India was still making the same primitive model (locally re-christened Ambassador), thanks to the restrictive policies of the government. Japan set an example for other East Asian tigers like Korea, Taiwan, Singapore and Hong Kong, who were seen as able junior partners by the Western world, while India languished in the category of poverty stricken, third world, developing nations.

But what really forced India's hand was that the neighboring China had started being mentioned by the Western world in endearing tones. A communist country was embracing open market economy, while as a democratic India was stuck with 'Socialistic' policies and a centralized planning apparatus. Gulf war in 1990s caused India's oil bill to swell so much that a 'Balance of Payment' crisis, which was on the horizon from mid-80s, precipitated in 1990. In Jan 1991, India was left with a foreign exchange reserves of US$ 1.2 billion (Wikipedia 1991, India economic crisis, 2012).

So, 1990s were wake-up call for India and the process of opening up started under the stewardship of Prime Ministers Rajiv Gandhi and later Narasimha Rao, and Dr. Manmohan Singh was co-opted as Finance Minister in this epic journey.

Let us start by tracing the rate of growth, as it accelerated as a result.

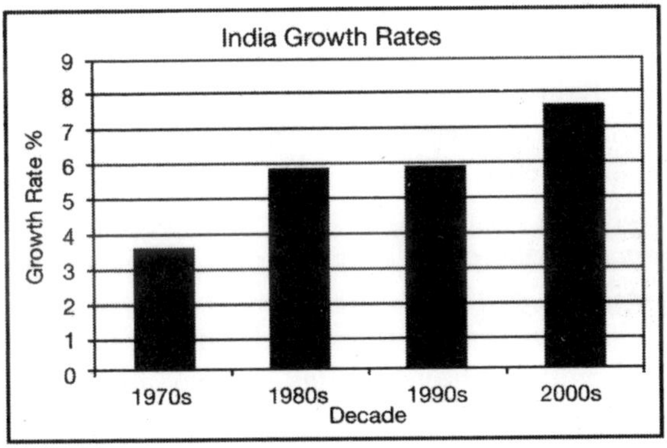


But loosening the stranglehold of license/permit Raj was hesitant and arduous. The politicians and the bureaucracy, long used to wielding the power of saying 'No' without being suitably rewarded at each step, would not let go of their leverage so fast or easily. The push/pull continues even today. Whenever there is a proposal for adapting to changing global requirements which entails removing the control of government over some industrial activity, the entrenched interest (politicians and bureaucracy who benefit from status quo) always drum up enough support to make the change slow, if not altogether impossible.

But wherever openness has been adopted, there has been tremendous acceleration in the industries, especially the domains where the government monopolies or reservations have been removed. Telecom is a shining example.

Then there were Luddites, who would spring up for maintaining status quo, under some pretext or the other. Sometimes, the logic forwarded would be that the change may not be compatible with the leanings of our past leaders or culture or even religious tenets. It was frustrating for the go getters sometimes, whenever they wanted to push forward; the Luddites would try to forestall their effort by pointing something in the backwards direction.

It is worth recalling a very interesting instance of the entrenched 'resistance to change'. It was proposed to computerize the banking system in the 1990s. In India those days, the banking industry was dominated by public sector banks, as after a second dose of nationalization in 1980, the Government of India controlled around 91 per cent of the banking business (Wikipedia, Banking in India 2012). The banking employees associations promptly went on strike, declaring the computerization will make banking staff redundant (and their lives difficult), so they wont let the equipment be installed and would boycott the call for training. The explanation that computerization is the need of hour for making banking industry achieve global standards, fell on deaf ears. Many years later, the banking industry has grown manifold and the incident forgotten. But in a democratic India, the rabble rousers always get to throw the spanner in the wheel first. It is later, with a lot of cajoling that you can build consensus and proceed. This is one major factor that 'the elephant can't run'.

Getting back to the growth rate in the graph, the opening up of the Indian economy immediately showed positive results and in the 1990s, the growth almost doubled to 6 per cent and then kept going up. Late 1990s saw appearance of one in a millennium chance (literally) in form of Y2K business opportunity. It not only heralded the beginning of a huge software services industry, but also bootstrapped the engagement of the Western countries with Indian private sector in many other domains like pharmaceuticals, telecom, healthcare, aviation, infrastructure, manufacturing, defense, etc. The comfort factor in working with Indians in combined teams saw metamorphosis. Soon there were ubiquitous arrangements of multi-site distributed teams and virtual teams in software development, knowledge services and R&D.

A progressive outward looking India has further expanded channels for cooperation through the auspices of WTO and has also through bilateral treaties based on mutual interests rather than 'lumped groups' arrangements forced by 'cold war' logic in earlier times. The Indian Diasporas have also contributed handsomely by adding their success stories to the script of Indian excellence.

The Y2K and software outsourcing success could finally nudge the Indian government to encourage this emerging industry. 'Software Technology Parks' scheme was one of the few enabler policy initiatives by a government that had earlier made a virtue out of controlling the industry rather than enabling it. As a result, software became a quickly increasing export and at >US$ 60 billion in 2010, was the largest component of Indian exports in the year. The engagement and comfort level between Indian software vendors and foreign multinationals also provided a robust platform for outsourced BPO (Business Process Outsourcing) services and lately KPO (Knowledge Process Outsourcing).

There is also a pointer in the IT story, to a fundamental difference between India and China. Indian economy is driven (by private sector entrepreneurs) despite the government, while Chinese economy is growing only because of the government (push).

The increasing breadth of outsourcing and skill level enhancement has pushed India on a higher growth trajectory. The rate exceeded 7.5 per cent after 2000 and has been in the range from 7.5 to 9 per cent till 2010. After the global financial crisis also, the rate is likely to be maintained above 7 per cent.

There are other dimensions that India has made great strides in. The international diplomacy, cultural linkages, environment protection, energy security, financial stability, healthcare and economic growth of Africa region are some of the activities that have seen increased participation by India in consonance with her larger profile in the world.

So much about the present status, let us now look forward and see what prognosis the future holds for India.

# 3

# A Peep into the Future of India

Having had a look at what India did (or whatever happened to India) in the past, now is the time to step up and look forward. Let us begin by believing what many have been analysing and assessing for the last few years. For this purpose, we use the causal analysis and forward projections data by some very established and able organizations. However, when trying to assume these projections as a reliable backdrop for my analysis, I am made somewhat tentative by the rather powerful and convincing assertions of Nassim Nicholas Taleb about 'Black Swans',

> the 'fat tails', that wild brand of uncertainty that causes large deviations (rare events that explain more and more of the world we live in, but at the same time remain as counterintuitive to us as they were to our ancestors. (*Fooled by Randomness*, Penguin Books, 2007, p. viii)

Our best option therefore is to accept these analyses and projections as more indicative than absolute in terms of figures and possibilities of achievement.

Nor can we not afford the time and effort to reinvent the wheel. So using the existing information base, we build our understanding and further thought process. But still heeding Taleb, we keep our mind open to possibility that uncertainty may be lurking around the corner and could modulate our inferences accordingly.

Let us get going then. We can look at various perspectives. How do we grow in terms of dollars? How do we induce Urban Growth? How are we placed in terms of human resources.... And so on.

We need to maintain a helicopter view of things. We are doing this analysis for finding out, what need be done to get India up there in future. But understanding of the topic will sometimes necessitate drilling down to details that seem removed from the main topic. Our best option is to maintain macro perspective for most time. Wherever required, we will drill down to micro level for a while, but will return to macro perspectives quickly, without losing focus. We can be assured that in the ensuing analysis, many lower level perspective have been synthesized in the background (with the help of an information model that will be described in later chapters) to create the cogent macro level views.

To begin, let us look at possibilities for size of economy first. Let us look at some reliable data presented in table form below:

## Economic Growth Projections

The size of the economy is the grandfather of all indications of a nation's progress. Let us see how it looks like for India.

**India's Ascent: The Projected Decadal Changes GDP**

| Year >>>> | 2010 | 2020 | 2030 | 2040 | 2050 |
|---|---|---|---|---|---|
| GDP US$ (PPP) constant 2009 international dollars), bn | 4067 | 8005 | 15292 | 25496 | 41374 |
| GDP per Capita (PPP) | 2645 | 5877 | 9977 | 15137 | 22886 |
| GDP (PPP) Increase | ---- | 3938 | 7287 | 10204 | 15878 |

**Challenges**

1. Policy evolution to keep up with geometric expansion
2. Financials: New modes of Investment and private sector push
3. Industrial infrastructure scaling
4. Educational and research renaissance.

*Source*: World Bank for 2009, PwC main scenario model projections for 2010-50

Wow. Doubling of GDP every 10 years! Can this happen? What is making it possible? Are there any 'ifs and buts' about it? If so, what could all be minimal 'sine qua non' for this to happen?

Let us have a look.

But firstly, another important point begs underlining. Forty years could be a just a blip in marathon of human history. But in the context of competition between nations in economic development, which can be likened to a 100 meters dash, it is rather a tall order to maintain persistence of economic growth, 'quarter after quarter' and year after year. Maintaining and scaling all parameters and enablers in equilibrium and synchronism for decades, is a Herculean task even for the best of advanced economies.

Let us take a measure of the India story.

1. From 2010 to 2020, the GDP will double from US$ 4 trillion (PPP) to US$ 8 trillion (PPP). That means that India's 50 years growth prior to 2010 will be replicated in just 10 years between 2010 and 2020. Catering for increased value delivery, efficiency and strengthening of currency even, the multiplication factor (over ten years) will be more than 1.5. That means that India will scale each of the factor inputs by approximately 1.5 times, i.e. 50 per cent more raw materials, workspace, trained workers, electricity, other utilities like transport communications, etc.
2. Between 2020 and 2030, the GDP almost doubles again. That means we add to GDP as much as twice the current economy size. That also means that we are replicating the progress or the previous 50 years yet again. The factor inputs have to be scaled up by 1.5 times again, i.e. whatever we added in the last ten years we need to add more than that now.
3. Between 2030 and 2040, we add to GDP as much as the 2.5 times the current GDP of India. Factor inputs now have to scale again by 1.5 times in 10 years. Now input factor creation is at another scale, and bears no

resemblance to the state of affairs in 2010. Concentration of factor creation is near clusters and has to be on decentralized basis to respond to ever changing business scenario.

4. Between 2040 and 2050, the addition is even steeper, i.e. four times the current GDP size. Factor inputs now have to scale again by 1.5 times in 10 years. Factor creation itself will become a huge high tech industry, changing the factor portfolio, scaling, inducting new technology as the industry portfolio changes and linkages between markets evolve. The overall business scenario is quite like decentralized sophisticated cluster systems in collaborative mode (cluster of clusters).

Can it be as simple as that? The first thing that comes to mind is all superlatives like gargantuan, astronomical and elephantine. I don't think we have a phrase called 'mathematical illusion' in dictionary. So let us try to understand these figures and how these came about on the analyst's tables.

As discussed earlier in this book, the Indian and Chinese economies have been major players in the global scene, till the Western economies discovered the magic wand of industrialization. To ensure the competitive advantage of technology and new processes/systems, the Western countries drove down the other economies to the status of raw material suppliers and ensconced themselves as sole proprietors of high tech (consequently high value) manufacturing. This exploitative regime continued till 'Black Swans' like Second World War arrived to shake the balance a little bit and then communication technology (especially internet) flattened the world by spreading the technical competence democratically. The latent capabilities of Indian technologists first came to fore with Y2K and then have kept climbing on the learning curve. Success spawns more success and the industrial roller coaster set in motion is now accelerating. To some extent, it is both push and pull. The pent up capabilities revealing themselves in context of India (and also other BRICS) and slowing down of Western economies have pushed India on a high rise trajectory.

So even if the projections look more geometric than additive, there is a comforting thought in the corner of the mind. Due to both push and pull factors, India's GDP has grown at a rate of 8 per cent or thereabouts without much of an effort by government or others in ruling elite, riding on the aggregate effort of a few millions (mostly in private sector) who have put their shoulder to the wheel. So if all stakeholders in India (government included) can make a concerted effort, the 'Horse may yet fly' (Due apologies to Taleb).

But frankly, this is still unbelievable. Can we have the number of companies delivering products and services (especially SMEs) increasing in a way that each kind of product/services doubles in value or is equivalently replaced by better ones? Can we educate and train the number of workers year after year for many decades? Can we have the investments to enable such a volume of industry, enablers and employment? Can we have skill enhancement (and R&D effort) for ever improving products, technology, services, delivery mechanisms, etc? Can we have the infrastructure scaling in a way to make all the above said possible? And the biggest 'if'; can our governance improve to facilitate all the above?

If we sift the media for economic information, China is likened to a 'Dragon' while India finds a simile in 'Elephant'. The sobriquet has been assigned because India progresses quite like a heavy, lumbering and non-aggressive pachyderm. To expect that this 'gentle giant' will suddenly sprout wings and take to the skies for a supersonic flight seems somewhat of a 'flight of fancy'. It certainly seems an anomaly with respect to its past character.

The big questions confronting us are,

1. Will we have a government which is an enabler rather than a 'spoke in the wheel'? Will we have laws, policy framework and procedures which will let the economy expand at such a breakneck speed, without having the industry queuing up at government offices for one matter or the other.

2. Who will put in the money? Will the government reduce its unproductive expenditure and invest more in industrial enablers? Will it provide incentives to private sector and FIIs to invest big in the expansion of industry?
3. Will the government invest in infrastructure or let infrastructure be scaled by non-government entities by instituting schemes and policy packages for such investments?
4. Will the government encourage education and research by policy liberalization and encouraging investment in private sector research and development by tax exemptions?
5. Will the government get down to its core business, i.e. providing policy support, security (business continuity assurance) from a multitude of factors (external threats, law and order, social unrest and diplomatic support in international negotiations, etc.).

Can all this happen at a fast pace? Are there any initiatives under way? Is something miraculous happening that is not public knowledge yet?

Let us let the matter rest for the time being and go look at another perspective for maybe a clearer look.

## Urban Growth

Urban growth has a recursive (two-way) cause-effect relationship with economic growth. If we see the rise of Europe in the nineteenth century, the industrialization and commercial growth resulted in urbanization push and in turn the urban centers of excellence became world leaders in commerce. London, Amsterdam, Venice in earlier times; and Hong Kong, Singapore and New York in recent times became big metros for the reason. And if you wanted to be a big player in global commerce, you had to do business in these cities, so these cities kept growing further by a snowballing effect. Similar process in respect of both commerce and manufacturing industry has been seen in China recently. Not only the old Chinese cities like Shanghai have grown to mega proportions, but new cities (where foundation stones were laid only 30 years back) have become big and centers of global business. Similar shift is underway in India too.

Let us step back and briefly uncover the rationale for the rural to urban shift. In earlier times, agriculture was the mainstream profession. With population growth, there has been a gradual increase of working hands that cannot be deployed in agriculture sector. So these extra hands have been pushed out to other professions. Mechanization of agriculture has accelerated the process further.

The pull factor has been industrialization. The concentrated form of industrial activity (plants, factories, mines, etc.), have provided these extra hands avenues for employment, though not in the vicinity of their earlier homes in the farming communities. So migration from rural to the new industrial towns and cities has coincided with the industrial progress.

We can see this shift in India also, as it rapidly industrializes. Indian landscape, which was 90 per cent rural and 10 per cent urban in 1947 at the time of partition, is irrevocably moving towards quick urbanization. The current rural/urban ratio is 70 per cent/30 per cent and India is expected to have more urban than rural population somewhere between 2040 and 2050.

But the big difference is that in India, the rural/urban migration has been more of a laissez-faire basis rather than a planned relocation. In fact we have one of the worst records in urban planning and infrastructure building. The urban slums are a testimony to the lack of any concerted effort for planned urbanization. All our big cities are a platter of ad hoc growth with private citizens trying to make do with whatever they can arrange for their living, and the government a mute spectator to their ever increasing travails.

Looking forward, the urban growth cannot be sustained with that kind of 'hands off' approach. Un-organized alleviation of the civic problems (setting aside unpopulated areas for dumps, using ground water, generating electricity for individual usage by portable generators, etc.), have already been exploited to the hilt (in addition to our cities looking like garbage dumps, these have created umpteen problems like health, pollution and of course poor living conditions).

So we need to ascertain the magnitude of the oncoming urban shift and plan and build urban infrastructure and other linkages unless we want to let Indian cities descend into chaos.

The table below shows the shift that is under way.

**India's Ascent: The Projected Decadal Changes: Urban Growth**

| | Year 2010 | 2020 | 2030 | 2040 | 2050 |
|---|---|---|---|---|---|
| Total Population Millions | 1214 | 1367 | 1485 | 1565 | 1615 |
| Urban Population Millions | 365 | 464 | 590 | 734 | 875 |
| Urban Population as per cent of Total Population | 30 | 34 | 40 | 47 | 54 |
| Urban Population Increase (Organic growth + Migration) Millions | ---- | 99 | 126 | 144 | 141 |

**Challenges**

1. Living/work space and civic amenities
2. Educational facilities
3. Health services
4. Entertainment and life improvement
5. Training and employment

*Source*: Population Division of the Department of Economic and Social Affairs of the United Nations Secretariat, World Population Prospects: The 2008 Revision and World Urbanization Prospects: The 2009 Revision, http://esa.un.org/wup2009/unup/

Now, to gauge the enormity of the task,

1. Between 2010 and 2020, 100 million people will move to the expanding old cities or new ones.
2. Between 2020 and 2030, the numbers moving in will be 126 million, next two decades will see about 140 millions each.

3. There is no let up in the rate of migration. So there has to be modular growth schema that allows scaling up without digging up the whole country that seems to be the current methodology (of urban development). For the purpose, the long-term planning and cascading project management models have to replace the current yearly budget and planning models. Staged, progressive, incremental, agile model (SPIAM) will have to be adopted rather than one shot component build model, which generally results in a nominal 50 per cent rework.
4. The technology, systems and processes will need constant upgrade and improvement, so it is essential that infrastructure development process is made as broadband as possible to get private sector, technology organizations, interest groups and opinion groups involved in creating functionally effective urbanization scenario.
5. The centralized system of urban development has to be replaced by decentralized system, so that there is continuous monitoring of the scaling up rather than once a year (hands off) budgetary allocation exercise.

So the big questions facing us are

1. Who will take up the ownership of urbanization? Who will plan, implement and optimize new and old cities keeping in tune with the rapid economic activity? Is the government ready to devolve power to local urban bodies? Can we follow the decentralized China model?
2. Who will plan and administer civic services, health and education, and staggered growth and continuous improvement of systems and processes. Can we corporatize the city management as in London or New York?
3. Who will establish health services, life-enrichment facilities, etc. Can we permit private sector in infrastructure sector without government intrusion?
4. Where will the funding come from? Will it be government controlled or private public partnership?

5. Who will create enabler services, e.g. electricity, water, communications, sewerage, garbage collection, local transportation, etc. Can all these be privatized?

Urban planning in India is a 'state controlled' centralized system, which is ineffective and leaky. Even for cities, the budgeting and sanctions are vested with the government at state capitals. The funding is very low (one sixth of levels in China, and there is no comparison at all with Western economies), and that too is wasted in fire-fighting (solving problems that pleases pressure groups but does nothing for the long-term growth/betterment of the cities) rather than creation of extra capacity. We are already hearing some negative impressions about our cities (dying city, dirtiest city and most polluted cities) and as such there is a requirement to incur a big one time investment to create the basic foundation for urban expansion and renewal. If we are not able to create a modular framework for our urban rejuvenation, there is hardly a chance that the economic projections can be realized.

There is yet another aspect related to complexity of initiatives. The complexity of an issue rises by the square principle. That is, if there are X parameters of a problem, the complexity level is proportional to $X^2$. So if the numbers of issues are doubled, the problem becomes four times more complex. The urban development problem is already complex, but it is very important to solve it as soon as possible before it becomes intractable or outright impossible. We need to use project management models (e.g. SPIAM, a Staged, Progressive, Iterative, Agile, project management method, a flexible management method for complex and long-term projects) that will let us manage complexity at various capacity levels, while allowing capacity expansion and quality/technology upgrade.

The alacrity that is required in this aspect is sorely missing in the governance domain, and the awareness totally missing in the general public.

### Work Age Population Increase

Human resources endowment is the critical factor in India's expected growth. It is an exclusive advantage amongst the BRICS nations that will work in India's favor through 2050.

The projected GDP growth will take place on increased industrial activity, for which we need to build infrastructure. But the most important factor input is the skill sets of workers that will create the value aggregating to the growing numbers of GDP. India is placed at an inflexion point in the history wherein the population in the working age range of 19 to 60 years will keep increasing, while rest of the world faces a severe crunch of hands, some of them facing depopulation (negative growth of population) as well. The problem is already critical in advance economies and China seems to be getting into that envelope in 10-15 years from now.

Strange as it may sound, India's strategic advantage of demographic boon is the result of failed 'Birth Control' policy of the Indian Government in 1960s and 1970s. Equally strange is the fact that China is facing this predicament because of their phenomenal success with 'One Child Policy' during similar periods.

The problem with demographic dividends is that they are many decades in the making. Another fact of nature is that demographic momentum is potent and requires huge amount of voluntary effort to change course.

Let us dwell on the demographic shift that is going to be a major factor in the changing global power equations in the coming future.

Let us take the case of India first. The average number of children per woman has been hovering around six for the period between 1900 and 1950. The major reasons were high children mortality in 0-5 year age range and overall low life expectancy (it was only 37 years in 1947). Consequently, it made sense to common folks to sire many children so that even if they lose a few, there were some to spare. The 1960s saw an effort to control the fertility rate, but there were more young mothers from earlier generation who with lesser (say 4) children could keep adding to population at rates similar to earlier decades. Now after 60 years, the rate of increase of population is dropping down (but now there are many more factors in play, e.g. higher female literacy, prosperity, improved healthcare and increased life expectancy).

For confirmation of this trend in demographic processes, that the population growth reduces as education, healthcare and prosperity increases, let us look at the case of advanced countries. The female literacy, prosperity and healthcare delivery systems have always been excellent there in the last 60 years. As a result, the fertility rate has been constantly coming down. At the turn of century, it has fallen below replacement rate (number of births are now less than the number of deaths). The government effort to encourage people to have more children, by exhortation of patriotic spirit, by facilitating child bearing (even paternity leave) and straight forward monetary rewards (gifts, children allowance, free education for children) has not arrested the fall of birth rate.

So as it stands, India has a great advantage of currently having larger percentage of its people in work age bracket than any other country. It is a boon that India will enjoy till 2050. The table below shows projections.

**India's Ascent: The Projected Decadal Changes Work Age Group Increase**

| Year >>>> | 2010 | 2020 | 2030 | 2040 | 2050 |
|---|---|---|---|---|---|
| Ratio Working/Non-Working | 1.8 | 2.1 | 2.2 | 2.3 | 2.15 |
| Urban Population (% of Total) | 30 | 34 | 40 | 47 | 54 |
| Working Age Population | 780 | 926 | 1021 | 1091 | 1102 |
| Working Age Population Increase | ---- | 146 | 95 | 70 | 12 |

**Challenges**

1. Urban infrastructure development
2. Industrial expansion, education and job opportunities
3. Cluster formation, consolidation for deployment of increased workforce
4. Conducive social environment

*Source*: United Nations (2009)

However, the demographic advantage does not convert to increase in GDP automatically. You have a lot of people that can lift our economy to the sky by aggregate effort. But before they can be productive, they have to be housed, clothed, fed, educated, trained and deployed on tasks that they can add value to. Each of these pre-requisite has to be met; otherwise this boon converts to a bane as quickly. If people don't have the basic necessities (and also life enrichment experiences) they will either turn to foul means for survival or become disenchanted and will disrupt the functioning of the society.

Let us look at the information in the table for ascertaining the challenges in encashing our demographic dividend.

1. We are adding almost 150 million workers to our work force between 2010 and 2020. Suffice to say that this additive number is more than half of the total workforce of European Union today.
2. Between 2020 and 2030, we will add about 100 million more. During the same period, the work age population in advance economies, Russia and even China would be shrinking.
3. Between 2030 and 2040, India will still add 70 million workers and 10 million more in the next 10 years.
4. Between 2010 and 2050, the ratio of working and non-working population steadily increases from 1.8 to 2.3, thus allowing India to exploit her human assets without getting bogged down for upkeep of graying population. Everywhere else in the advanced world, the ratio drifts to 1.2 and lower. Russia, Western Europe, Japan would have shrinking populations as well to add to the woes of a large dependent senior society.
5. With industrialization apace, these extra numbers are adding to the urban areas especially around cluster of industries, i.e. tier 1 and tier 2 cities.
6. We need to enroll additional 10 million people each year through our basic education system, and at least a million a year through professional education. Currently 90 per cent of 226 million children of school going age

are enrolled in the primary schools, but the effectiveness of the schooling system leaves much to be desired. Dropout rate before finishing primary education is 40 per cent and before finishing high school is >50 per cent. We need to create technical education training to raise our technical manpower as a percentage of population (per 1000 figures currently are, India/3.5, China/8.1, South Korea/46, Israel/76, and Japan/110). We need to at least double our graduating engineers from 600,000 to 1.2 million to catch up with the world as well as to keep our growth on track. We need a policy recast for substantive investment in education.

7. As the Indian economy progresses from a developing to an emerging and onwards to a developed status, there will be a need to raise the standards of education and research to 'state of the art' and leadership levels. That will require academia to play a major part and national policies to empower the academia to achieve global standards. Our research investment is paltry 0.9 per cent of GDP as compared to 3 per cent in the advance economies. High tech MNC organizations spend as much as 11 per cent of revenues in R&D for new product development. India is too dependent on imported technology and lacking in R&D. This has to change.
8. As urbanization increases the population density in new towns and cities, the social mores change. Life sustenance (civic amenities) and enrichment (entertainment, culture and social activities) get reconfigured. The urban environment has to keep evolving and that can happen if and only if, the local citizens and the local government have a major play in the urban administration. Both investment and policy push are required.
9. Integrated commercial, industrial and domestic urban development is the only way forward for mega cities of tomorrow.

So the questions facing us are

1. Will the policy framework change from paternalistic to enabler?
2. Will the education outlay ever increase from 4 per cent or there about. Many commissions have recommended hiking outlay by 50 per cent at least. Will it happen now?
3. Would the capacity augmentation and quality upgrade in education system be encouraged by privatization?
4. Will we be able to expand our range and depth of R&D effort qualitatively and quantitatively in academia and industry? Will we try to emulate advance economies and organizations in R&D?

## Increased Productivity

The intangible but a very important aspect of transformation of Indian economy from a developing to leadership role is likely to be the productivity and efficiency improvement alongside physical (GDP, Infrastructure, human resources) expansion.

*[Another factor could be brand equity fillip (manifesting as currency appreciation) but we have already equalized that effect by measuring GDP on PPP basis with a base 2009 dollars].*

The GDP is forecasted to expand by a factor of 10 while the workforce is to expand by a factor of 1.5. Thus, growth has to come from increasing value addition per worker. There are a couple of underlying shifts that we can see taking place in Indian economy, that will result in higher productivity.

1. Continuing transformation of agro based economy to industrial economy.
2. From raw material supplier to sub-system supplier and onwards to system supplier.
3. From technology importer to self sufficiency and then technology exporter.
4. From commodity exporter to high value exporter and commodity importer.

The aggregate effect of the four abovementioned transformations will manifest in gradual increase the average productivity per worker in the Indian economy. The productivity scaling is captured in the table below,

*(Data courtesy World Bank for 2009, PwC main scenario model projections for 2010-2050)*

**India's Ascent: The Projected Decadal Changes Increased Productivity**

| | 2010 | 2020 | Year 2030 | 2040 | 2050 |
|---|---|---|---|---|---|
| Productivity US$ (PPP) | 5211 | 8644 | 14978 | 23375 | 37534 |
| Productivity Increase US$ (PPP) | ---- | 3433 | 6334 | 8396 | 14160 |

**Challenges**

1. Industry evolution to high tech
2. Skill set growth to high value
3. Associated upgrade of regulatory environment.

*Source*: Calculated GDP/Worker Ratio

The productivity per worker is projected to increase by a factor of just less than 2 each decade from 2010 to 2050. Productivity is a multiple of three factors namely,

- Worker skills (blue collar, white collar, high tech).
- Systems and technology (process excellence, quality and precision, niche tech).
- Market development level (product acceptance).

To state the obvious, advance economies have larger proportions of high value products and services. It is not that advance nations don't grow vegetables. But they produce a larger percentage of (global output) aircraft than cauliflowers. Similarly they achieve better efficiencies and quicker processes. Japan buys coal and iron ore from India and others, pays for shipping costs for high volume raw materials, manufactures steel and still competes in the world markets for selling high class steel. It is because they use less energy per ton of steel and have their processes so finely tuned that they can meet customers requirements anywhere in the world within a stipulated timeframe. And of course, the industry has to ascertain the market requirements before they go on to mass produce. If you are not able to realize revenues, productivity does not include the stuff in the junkyard.

A related factor in productivity rise is the regulatory environment. There are new processes, new technologies, new business models, new sources of raw materials and new markets. If the Governing bodies are facilitators in these matters (like Singapore government), the productivity gains are easier to realize. If for each change, the governing bodies are an obstacle (requiring permissions, explanations, denials, delays, procedural wrangles), the business entities will land up queuing in front of government offices rather than responding to change.

It is interesting to see how US business colossus and technological superiority was built. There are two kinds of main players in the US rise to supremacy. First kind is the big corporations with deep pockets and staying power. These big players are generally multi-domain players and have staying power to take the lows and highs and can shuffle their portfolios like a pack of cards. The second kind is SME (small and medium enterprises), basically smart and bright young technologists, who have a winning idea and are ready to bet on it with their lives. They generally come in twos or fours and sometimes their ideas can interest the venture capitalists (VCs). VCs themselves are a different breed. They are people who have a lot of money that they want to deploy for quick and big gains.

Only one out of ten ventures reaches some kind of maturity that gives the entrepreneurs and VCs substantial gains. But as long as the gains are in multiples of hundreds, the VCs have succeeded and so do the entrepreneurs. For the other nine, liquidation is the way generally and bankruptcy is a quick and not a very cumbersome procedure in US. That means, this failure is put behind and the entrepreneurs are able to reenter market again with a clean slate. There is no stigma in failing once or twice. But there is stigma attached to not trying again.

These SMEs are founts of new technology products/services/processes for the big league commercial organizations. They bring new ideas to the market and their contribution to innovation is widely acknowledged. They are generally acquired and merged with big commercial organizations and their technology internalized by the acquiring organization. Some start ups are able to achieve exponential growth and become behemoths by themselves. Microsoft and Google are these success stories. Commercial organizations as well as the governments keep a lookout for new innovations and systems in the SME segment.

In contrast to the popular song, which rhymes "This happens only in India", "This does not happen in India". We are not yet an entrepreneurial nation at grass-root level (though I have met many IIT/IIM stalwarts starting the trend in social sector). While as 65 per cent of economic output in Europe is by SMEs and 45 per cent in US (by 24 million SMEs), Indian SMEs create only 17 per cent (survey by ASSOCHAM, 2011) of GDP and that too is not in innovative high tech field. It is estimated that 80 per cent of the innovations take place at SME level (large organizations have too much bureaucracy to allow unfettered creativity). So unless we have venture capital and entrepreneurship taking root in India, we will be severely constrained to become self-sufficient in technology prowess, much less become technology leaders and exporters.

It seems to be a strange that the Indian government has no focus on SMEs. No policy support, no financial environment for SMEs to prosper and (most strangely) no procurement from SMEs (in fact most of the qualification criteria for procurement rule out SMEs by setting a high revenue threshold). Strangely, in India, SMEs are looked at as entities requiring government support for survival, rather than the founts of industrial innovation.

To have India in the top league, 'it will have to happen in India'. And it can happen only if regulatory environment undergoes change (policies that allow SMEs to start and exit business without prolonged procedures, allow startups tax breaks for the initial phase, financial support from government and banks before venture capital takes root, high tech procurement from SMEs, etc.).

So the big questions are

1. Will the government take policy initiatives in encouraging entrepreneurship?
2. Will there be enough activity at SME level to expand our innovation effort to a wide area in our industrial activity?
3. Will we have venture capitalist who will invest money despite the risk profile of these SMEs?
4. Will the big industry houses or big users (like government, defense, homeland security, transportation, etc.) pursue a strategy of encouraging R&D in the country rather than continuing dependence on import of technology (development projects and new technology usage has to become a part of strategy for these organizations for the purpose)?

To summarize

1. India is on the path of explosive growth, helped both by push as well as pull factors. Slowing of advance economies, graying of Western countries and Japan (later China) and dismantling of technology exclusivity regime are the external factors. Advancement of education and technology (partly kicked off by Y2K and partly because of long-term plans), demographic dividend and democratic institutions being the internal factors.
2. Growth is not a given. It is only a 'window of opportunity', but a window with a huge possibility. It is also a strictly 'time bound' opportunity. There are many challenges that are required to be overcome before the possible projections of India's GDP rise can be realized.
3. The current state of affairs (policies and plans, governance, infrastructure, processes and systems) is

not the one that will take us to the top of the table. India has a big 'To Do' list.

4. Looking at the opportunity as 'Once in our living history', India and Indians can put up a multi-dimensional effort to realize our potential (we have missed many a bus earlier due to a plethora of reasons). The efforts will run parallel on four planes, namely
    a. Policy, plans, governance and financing.
    b. Building business environment, economy and technology.
    c. Infrastructure build and management.
    d. Skill repertoire scaling.
    e. Technology development and application to all domains.

But are we ready?

Let us take a stock of our capabilities or readiness for each of these next.

# 4

# Monitoring India's Rise: Indicators, Enablers and Show-stoppers: Putting them Together: The Concept of a Dashboard

We have already given ourselves a feel of the upcoming growth story of India. Our ability to seize the opportunity will depend upon (i) the clarity of our thought, (ii) our aggregate will, (iii) our deliberate actions and (iv) the global environment. Now we take the next step towards clearly defining the issues in greater detail.

So shifting gears, we graduate from generic thoughts to specifics. We start by identifying the various facets that can accelerate or hinder India's growth. Further we need to introduce a way to measure the efficacy of these facets to ascertain India's current capability, and institute a generic action plan to achieve the projected growth.

Let us for a moment assume the mantle of India's planners and try to devise an approach that will allow us to monitor and analyze macro indicators, assess and visualize 'actions required' targets. If the targets are in words and figures (measurable), then we can use the same as a reference to measure compliance to plans, i.e. did things happen as envisaged?

As we have repeatedly resolved to keep things simple, this approach schema shall not be too complicated and yet would capture the core essence of the strategic planning process for India's growth.

So, we do two things.

Firstly, we build a parametric model that enumerates important constituent elements that have been hinted at previously. We organize them in a hierarchical structure of 'Strategy Areas', major 'Positive and Negative Factors' and their component 'Sub-factors'. The hierarchical tree structure can show us dependencies and relationships. And also enable us to find ways to ascertain the composite effect of micro issues (sub-factors) by merging them into intermediate level issues (factors) and similarly merging factors into macro issues (strategic areas).

The model scheme looks like as follows,

Status of India's progress

⇩

5 Strategy Areas

⇩

5 positive and 5 negative factors for each of the strategy areas

⇩

5 Sub-factors of each of the positive and negative factors

Secondly, using this schema we will create a simple mathematical model to assign and compute the efficacy values of sub-factors, factors and strategy areas. We want to create a bulletin board, which can provide us an easy to understand pictorial display of these parametric values, and point us towards actions that will allow us to improve/ameliorate the consequent (positive/negative) parametric effects.

For the purpose, we introduce the concept of a 'Dashboard'. A Dashboard is a graphic representation of the macro level parameters, i.e. of strategy area efficacy and factor values. The factor values are displayed as vertical bars and the strategy area efficacy is shown as figures in data windows on the Dashboard.

The name Dashboard underlines the intent that we want to understand the whole picture of India's progress by looking at this single display (akin to an automobile Dashboard that includes all displays that help us drive).

To keep the display from being cluttered, we hide all the underlying data and computations, so that we are not distracted from our basic theme, i.e. discussion on the Rise of India.

Let us first preview what the Dashboard looks like. And then we proceed to find out the import of displayed elements in detail before we can start interpreting the display.

The proposed Dashboard looks like as follows:

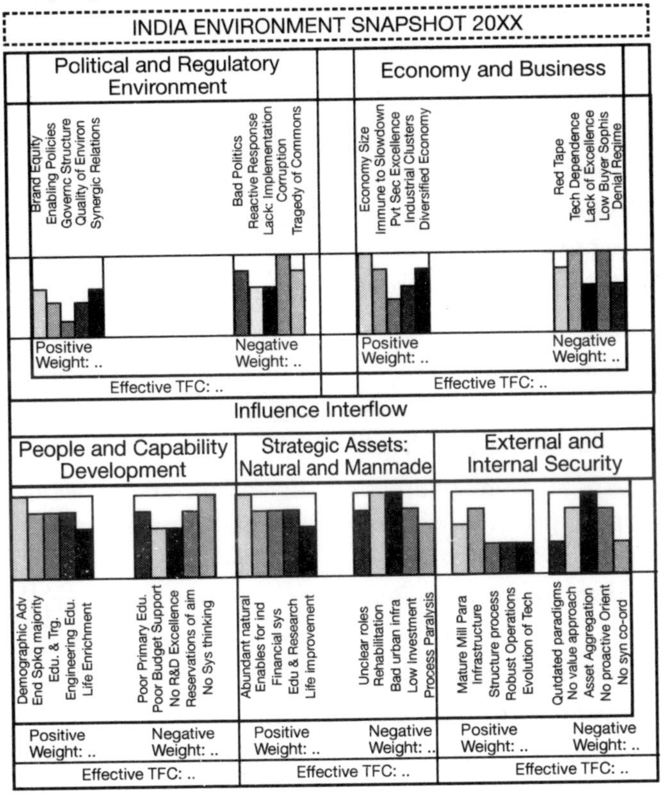


The Dashboard has five sections one for each strategy area. Each of these sections has bar displays for five positive factors (on the left side) and five negative factors. Each factor can have a value between one and five. In the data window below the positive factors is the alphanumeric value of composite weight of all positive factors. Similarly there is a data window for display of composite weight of all negative factors. The data window marked TFC displays the 'Total Factor Contribution' for that strategy area, i.e. difference between positive weight and negative weight.

So, one look on the Dashboard, and we can get the answers to the following queries:

1. What is the state of each factor in all strategy areas?
2. Are some factors begging immediate attention? (Low value of positive factors or high value of negative factors.)
3. What is the aggregate effect of positive factors in each strategy area?
4. Is it low? If yes, then what are the target areas for improvement?
5. What is the aggregate effect of negative factors in that strategy area?
6. If it is high, then what are the problem areas?
7. Do the positive factors overcome the negative factors?
8. If yes, by how much? Can we improve it further?
9. If no, are we spending more time in negative domain (alleviating problems)?
10. Are all strategy areas equally balanced? Do we need to pay special attention to certain strategy areas?
11. Do we have a strategic advantage in some strategy area that can be exploited for competitive advantage?
12. Do we have strategic constraint in some strategy area that we need to find an antidote or balancing factor for?

## Dashboard Information Components

*Statutory Warning* **1:** [The Dashboard presentation is built upon the information model, including strategy areas, factors, sub-factors, their inter relationships, methodology of their aggregation and then interpretation of the resultant value. We can begin to interpret the display without delving too deep into the information model of computation method. For the purist however, the details are available in Appendix "A" on Macro Information model and Appendix "B" on Micro Information model and computation Schema.]

***Statutory Warning* 2:** This exercise is for us, the non-experts to understand the whole gamut of India's rise in future. No claim is made that this schema could be used instead of elaborate planning by the responsible functionaries.]

Let us begin naming the major components of the dashboard stencil.

In keeping with our thought process in the foregoing discussion, the five macro target areas of our approach strategy are

A. Political and Regulatory Environment

B. Economy and Business

C. People and Capability Development

D. Strategic Assets: Natural and Manmade Resources

E. External and Internal Security

We had not yet brought in the security aspect in our discussion. But it is pertinent to introduce it now. The 'continuity assurance' for the other four strategy areas depends upon security. Also, the security forces are major consumers of high technology systems, information infrastructure and associated support services. So both as continuity assurors and big consumers, we need to include them in the big picture.

We are still constrained to leave out many important aspects like environmental issues and inclusive growth. These topics are important enough to merit a discussion separately. Let us stick to our aim of keeping it simple and concise, with a certain assurance that these aspects will be a part of a more detailed 'Project Plan' for 'India Rising' project.

For each strategy area, we enumerate five important factors that will show up as 'must do' items on any plan at macro level. A non-expert should be able to look at the presence and quality of these elements to gauge whether a particular element is contributing adequately to the progress of India. These factors are called positive factors. We should also be able to identify the five most onerous risk factors that can thwart India's march. These will be shown as positive/negative factor bars on the dashboard.

Just to underline, for the sake of brevity, we have chosen to enumerate the five most important positive factors and similarly the most important five negative factors. We follow the Pareto principle here, hoping that five factors each will capture the predominant (>80 per cent) character of the target area.

The basic thought process and the building up of pictorial representation of the five strategic areas is given in Appendix-A.

There is one important point that we are not including in our discussion, because we would overly complicate the 'concept' itself. The influence interplay window in our 'Dashboard' displays indicates that factors do not exist in silos, but we will ignore their interrelationships for the sake of simplicity.

### Drilling Down to Sub Factors, and Value Computations

We do want an 'easy to understand' analysis and discussion on the issues at hand, but we cannot run the risk of reaching the wrong conclusion for the sake of simplicity. So we need to drill down to finer granularity for getting a better accuracy of factor evaluation, i.e. further break down factors into sub-factors for ensuring that most micro level issues are included in our factor definition and estimation.

However, to avoid getting drowned the details, we provide the in depth sub-factor structure, weights and computation schema in Appendix "B".

For our analysis, it will suffice for us to know that we have assigned values to sub-factors, aggregated them to factors, further aggregation to positive and negative factor weights and finally computed total factor contribution for each strategy area.

It goes without saying that for becoming a world leader, you should carry more positive weight (literally) in every strategy area. At least, one should be 'best in class' or thereabout for being up there.

### Interpreting Our Dashboard

[The value shown now are only for explaining the stencil, we will come to real values later.]

Having understood the Dashboard display format, we are now ready to start interpreting the Dashboard.

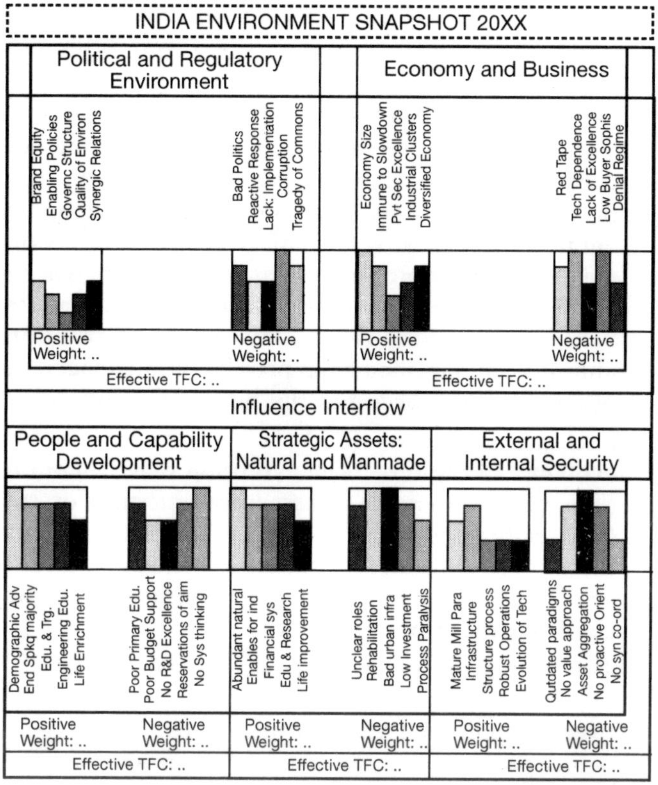


Let us ascertain how the 'Dashboard' will provide us the snapshot of India's progress at a selected epoch. The logic described below will assist in making the interpretation objective and focused.

1. The relative importance of each strategy area is different for different nations. It depends on the disposition of their resources, cultural preferences or maybe even the history of their successes. In case of India (for that matter all big nations), all these areas are important, only the relative importance varies.
2. For a particular nation, the relative importance of each strategy area is situation and time dependent. In conflict situations, the security and political dimensions have pre-eminence. In a competitive economic scenario; economy, resource development and people issues take

the lead. [But we are still talking long-term here, in terms of decades rather than years, war situations like Gulf region, or between India and Pakistan do have perspectives lasting half a century or more.]

3. The five factors in each strategy area are intended to capture 80 per cent of the core efficacy, but the proportion may vary from one stage of development to another. In early stages of development, corruption may be the more important issue, but reaching a developed state in economy (very much like the state of Scandinavian countries today, where corruption has almost been banished from peoples' mind-space), quality of environment becomes the basic differentiator.
4. Each of the factors (and their sub-factors in turn) is evolving all the time. The evolution may be continuous (like improvement in urban infrastructure) or stepped (like policy changes). The overall factor dynamics therefore will be a sort of multi-dimensional 'breathing' envelope, changing in various dimensions as well as changing the mix in the core.
5. The amplitude of positive weights of factors in each area is important by themselves. It represents the overall quality of that strategy area. You expect this value growing as the nation progresses and builds capability in that strategy area. One could (on first approximation), say that a positive weight of two would indicate backwardness, three a developing status and four onwards as a nation on the rising curve.
6. The differential between the positive weight and the negative weight is equally important. If the negative weight is appreciably more than positive weight (one or higher differential), then we are looking at a strategy area, where there are very serious problems. Positive weight marginally higher than negative weight indicates that there are serious challenges to be surmounted before the smooth rising curve can be achieved. A differential of two or more denotes a smoothly running developed nation state.
7. The challenge for the decision makers is maintaining each of the factors in a state that this differential is

always building up to a more positive aggregate and balancing and nudging factors to ensure that the slope always remains positive.

8. This 'continuous improvement' challenge can be met with continuous 'planning, implementing, monitoring, balancing, focusing, and synchronizing' cycle in a multitude of target areas but all the time varying focus and intensity of effort.

## Progress Dashboard, India 2010

The Dashboard for India in the year 2010 looks as follows:

[Note: Influence interflow window is intended to capture the inter-strategy dependencies, e.g., economy strength may influence security strategy and political environment may influence security environment. For the time being, for the sake of brevity, we postpone the assessment of interflows for later.]

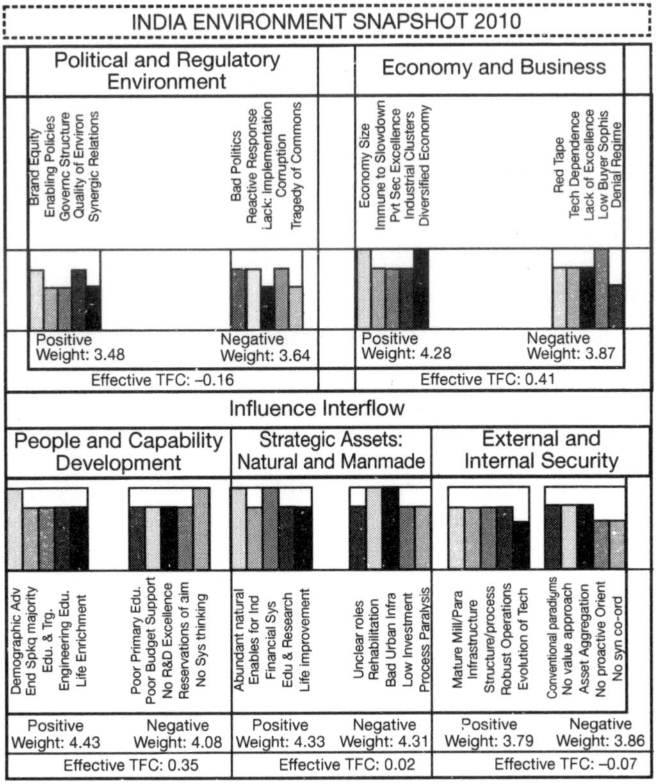

First some generic interpretations before we start with analysis of the India's competitive position in 2010.

**Observations: India 2010**

1. The positive weights in Economy, People and Assets areas are above 4. This indicates large endowment in current state of Indian Economy, demography and natural and cultural assets.
2. India is comparatively (as compared to the other three factors) lacking in political and military prowess.
3. The negative weights in 'Political and Regulatory Environment' and 'External and Internal Security' areas outweigh the positive weights. The indication is that these areas have more challenges than the other three.
4. All areas positive and negative factor weights are close in values. That indicates that India is still not in the big league. We need all-round improvements in multiple areas to get to a leadership position.
5. The most important positive factors needing a boost at this juncture are
   (a) Enabling Policy Framework (Political and Regulatory Environment)
   (b) Governance Structure (Political and Regulatory Environment)
   (c) Synergistic Relationships (Political and Regulatory Environment)
   (d) Development of Industrial Clusters (Economy and Business)
   (e) Education and Training (People and Capability Development)
   (f) Enablers for Industry, Urban Development, infrastructure (Strategic Assets: Natural and Manmade)
   (g) Education and research (Strategic Assets: Natural and Manmade)

   (h) Evolution of Technology (External and Internal Security).

6. The most important negative factors needing a quick amelioration at this juncture are
   (a) Bad Politics (Political and Regulatory Environment)
   (b) Corruption (Political and Regulatory Environment)
   (c) Tragedy of the Commons (Political and Regulatory Environment)
   (d) Red Tape (Economy and Business)
   (e) Technology Dependency (Economy and Business)
   (f) Low Buyer Sophistication (Economy and Business)
   (g) Poor Primary Education (People and Capability Development)
   (h) Reservations without Aim (People and Capability Development)
   (i) Lack of Systems Thinking: 'Jugaad' (People and Capability Development)
   (j) Rehabilitation (Strategic Assets, Natural and Manmade)
   (k) Urban Infrastructure (Strategic Assets, Natural and Manmade)
   (l) Value Approach Missing (External and Internal Security)
   (m) Asset Aggregation Mindset (External and Internal Security)
   (n) Pro-Active Reorientation Lacking (External and Internal Security)

In keeping with almost equal positive and negative weights (that shows good potential but weighed down with problems and challenges), we have lesser number of areas that could boost India's progress, but more negative areas that could pull it down.

We should note another point here. A nation's capabilities (very much like that of an individual) consist of two parts. One part that is given (inherits or endowed or is born with) and the other is what that nation makes of the endowment. Strategic areas include both the parts. Assets and demography is a nation's inheritance or gift of God. How that nation leverages is the second part. There are no guarantees the nations with rich endowment will always progress (Africa with its bagful of natural bounties is at the bottom of the progress ladder). But they can change it if they supplement there endowment with progress along other strategy areas. But it is possible to offset a part of the asset penury by excelling in the non-endowment areas (e.g., Human Development, Politics and Regulatory environment). Japan is a fitting example, that despite being poor in natural resources (and in addition being saddled with a perpetual natural disaster prone geography), they have set new standards in progress.

In Indian context, we have rich endowment of natural resources and demography at this juncture of time. In fact our demographic advantage is exclusive for the next 50 years or so. If we cannot leverage it, it will be because of a lot of negative performance in other strategy areas.

The Dashboard 2010 does give indications in that direction. We have also enumerated the possible factors that could be standing in the way of our leveraging our singular advantage at these times.

What we will see in the future, say in the year 2050, will depend upon how we push the positive factors and ameliorate/ obviate the negative ones. Next, let us see the two extreme possibilities that we could face in the year 2050.

# 5

# Monitoring India's Rise: Dream Scenario 2050

## 31 March 2050

It is an epoch (No I am not talking about India becoming a 100 trillion dollar economy or Inter-India Aviation declaring its first 30 billion quarter). It is the time for me to validate my India rising hypothesis. What an ego salve it is for humans, even more for the egoistic financial experts, to turn back and say, 'I told you so, Didn't I?'. (Please pardon the sentence formation, it had to start with an "I" and end likewise.)

Well, in 2010, we made some predictions (astrologers, excuse please), that India is going to get to a place of prominence in world affairs in the coming half century. That was forty years back and most of those projections (and more) have not only been realized, but some have been exceeded. Like they say a lot of water has flown down the Ganges (and other rivers too, though many rivers like 'Yamuna' and 'Beas' have run dry meanwhile), so it isn't a bad idea to look at some of the major things that took place in the last forty years.

## Politics and International Affairs

1. India finally became a UN Security Council member and the first IMF Chief from India took office in 2017.
2. India and China became co-chair of the World Economy Stabilization Program in 2021 after five European countries defaulted on loan commitments and the Euro zone was remodeled. The WESP now has its representatives in all major European capitals, advising these nations on the belt tightening measures to get their economy to turn around.

3. LECC (Large Economies Cooperation Council) expanded its membership to 12 after the entry of Nigeria, Saudi Arabia and Egypt. Now the group includes all the trillion dollar economies. USA and Germany continue to have observer status at all LECC meetings.
4. Indian political makeover that started in the 2020s has matured now, with the 'two party system' providing the much needed stability without getting distracted by non-issues. The two mainstream parties (Desh Bhakt Party and Sarv Jan Party) have stuck to their earlier resolve of sticking to economic and progressive agendas and stay away from divisive politics. The House of Lords (named so because most of its elected members were there either because of inheritance or money power) has been renamed Lok Sabha. The current polity represents the intelligentsia of the nation.
5. In India, there is a vigorous competition between states to get ahead in economic development. It started with Delhi-Mumbai industrial corridor implementation in 2020s (this spawned the now mega cities of Motinagar in Rajasthan and Atalgiri in Maharashtra). But not be left behind, the Delhi-Kolkatta corridor, with new projects in Bundelkhand and Bihar in 2030s; have set a new standard for integrated planning and implementation for steel and power industry. Lately, the coastal garland project that will focus on Odisa and Telangana areas, is the next big thing. The project is being eyed by IIIs (Indian Institutional Investors) and foreign equity funds.

## Economy and Business

6. India became the largest economy of the world in the year 2048. Its growth rate has been consistently above 5 per cent for the last decade, which is commendable, considering that other BRICS have slowed down to an average 3 per cent growth during the same time.

7. India became the largest donor to Africa Development Fund in 2042. The Indian contribution is being considered the catalyst for turn around of middle African region in 2040s.
8. India became the largest steel producer of the world in 2038. It has the largest aviation industry after US and China.
9. Indian defense industry has come in its own after the government initiative to reverse 70/30 mix of imported/indigenous procurement to 30/70 by 2035. In 2048, 90 per cent of the Indian defense acquisition against global tenders was from Indian MNCs. And these organizations were exporting 40 per cent of their products and services. Indian MNCs have a large market share for UAVs, Information systems and other 'Command and Control' components.
10. India became the largest destination of investment by FIIs, specially the pension funds because of steady returns and stability of the market. In 2040s, the average investment inflows were above US$ 25 billion each year. In addition M&A by Indian MNCs in China and US averaged US$ 11 billion each year, cementing the Indian supremacy in steel, automobiles and aviation manufacturing.
11. The Industrial clusters in Bangalore, Noida, Gurgaon, Pune, new Hyderabad, Coimbatore and Indore after the reconfiguration drive of 2032 have now been classified Gold Class in environmental protection and 'quality of life' assessment.
12. The aviation industry, which was in doldrums in mid-2010s, has now been put in a competitive position by some bold initiatives. National airspace management system, a billion dollar effort has made the traffic flow efficient that the fuel savings of up to 20 per cent have accrued to participating airlines. In addition, synchronized logistics hubs at Amritsar, Noida, Nagpur, Mumbai (the second airfield), Chennai, Guwahati and

Kolkatta have made the freight operations efficient and viable.

13. FDI policy 2017 has increased the comfort level for foreign businesses to invest in India. Specially manufacturing sector, after the Chinese cost advantage has worn off due to appreciating Renminbi, the electronics manufacturing hubs at Chandigarh and Bhopal have attracted a lot of contract manufacturing organization. Gurgaon and nearby Rajasthan Industrial Development township at Bhiwadi have also attracted consumer durable manufacturers.

14. The clustering of industries around focal points is very discernible and a policy driver for the government, both central and at state level. The IT industry, that was centered around Bangalore, Delhi, Hyderabad and Pune, is now more democratically dispersed. The new IT hubs at Shillong, Darjeeling, Indore, Baroda, Bhopal and Manipur are thriving in providing IT/knowledge services to new markets, especially China and East Asia. The new Aviation hubs at Nagpur and Hissar are developing at a tremendous pace too. Nagpur is likely to become the biggest maintenance base for Boeing, Bomardier and Airbus aircraft soon. Manufacturing has also taking root in Jamshedpur, Gandhinagar and Bhuvaneshwar clusters, with a high volume of auto and appliances industry establishing their manufacturing units there.

### People and Capability Development

15. There has been a renaissance in engineering education, after the 'distributed learning' plan of central government was kicked off in 2025. Now there are institutions of repute (IITs and AIIMS) in each of the 30 states. There has been a lot of interest in the foreign institutions of high learning (Harvard, Stanford, Imperial and IMD being the first movers in 2020s), to set up campuses in the readymade educational clusters that came up in Thanjavur, Palghat, Mysore, Manipur,

Patna, Mathura, Patiala and Nagpur. There are exchange programs with almost all institutions of repute in the world including the Chinese gold class universities.

16. The primary education coverage reached 98 per cent in 2030. Indian universities now produce two million engineers and scientists each year for its industry. Industry employs 1 per cent of its workforce for research and development now. These two million R&D workforce is at the forefront of new technology and innovative product development. In 2045 India became the topmost new patents nation.

### Strategic Assets: Natural and Manmade

17. 'Integrated urban planning and uplift' Law, 2018, that made it mandatory for all state governments to follow the basic guidelines of sustainable growth and 'quality of life' assurance, has been a critical catalyst in the urban renewal of old cities, and the birth of ultra modern cities like Gaurav Nagar in Bundelkhand and Pragati Yug in Assam. The devolution of powers to city corporations in 2021 under this law has underwritten the transformation of India's cities to the current level of development.
18. The investment in urban development, which saw an upward trend in 2020s, has been stepped up steadily especially for the decongestion and renewal programs. The IUPU guidelines that have ensured that a large percentage of city revenues are employed for upkeep and improvement has been instrumental for metamorphosis of all major cities.
19. Public Private Partnership for new cities has been a resounding success. In fact, two mega cities, Viratnagar in Madhya Pradesh and Rajnipalli in Tamilnadu, that have been developed exclusively by private partnerships and the state governments are a minor shareholder in most real estate projects and civic services. In these cities, power, communication, transportation, health

services and conservancy services are in private sector domain.

20. Sixteen cities in India now have annual budgets exceeding US$ 1 billion. The corporations, with elected Mayors at the helm, are run more as commercial corporations. The Mayors being constantly visible have a challenging job, but successful mayors are also becoming national level political stars.
21. The major rivers in India have received special attention 2030 onwards. The cleaning of the water sources (removing polluting industry from riverbank areas and making refuse treatment a legal responsibility) has done wonders to quality of water. The first time, water transportation system was developed for stretches of Ganges and Damodar between major industrial cities in 2035.
22. The Indian landscape, that was considered a display of chaos and penury by media, has suddenly been discovered for its vibrancy and multi-dimensional beauty. The tourists now are as eager to see the natural beauty of India as much to learn how to do business like Indians. The historical monuments at Agra, Rajasthan, Karnataka, Goa and many other states are attracting tourists in millions. In addition, the lower Himalayas have become a magnet for tourists wanting to enjoy the serenity and variety of flora and fauna in these enchanting foothills. Valley of flowers in Uttrakhand, Nilgiri Hills, Nagaland and Manipur are the new destinations that have been rediscovered. In addition the old favorites like Kerala backwaters, Goa beaches and deserts of western Rajasthan remain the popular winter haunts. Indian cities are now becoming magnets for international tourists not only for historical monuments, but also for shopping and quality of life. India hosted 23 million tourists in 2048 and along with business visitors; the total number of arrivals in India topped 30 million.

## External and Internal Security

23. Since 2020, the Defense modernization has proceeded continuously with an aim to create a force with capability of global reach. The new paradigms of quick reaction and integrated force modules have been helped by induction of 'state of the art' technology. The Indian defense forces are now considered to be in the top three in the world in terms of global footprint and effective capability.
24. India's borders and boundaries are now guarded by paramilitary forces with 24 × 7 systems and a combination of ground, satellite and UAV based sensors. The quick reaction teams with both fixed and rotary wing transports are able to react to any exigencies. The police forces have been able to bring down the crime rate especially in the new mega cities by using the new street based video surveillance systems.
25. India has taken a leap forward in maintaining peace at its borders by getting into pacts and understanding with its immediate neighbors and other nations in the region. That has helped India to employ its military resources for other trouble spots in the world.
26. Private sector is now actively engaged with defense services for development, integration and lifecycle support of systems. There are two aviation companies producing a wide variety of fighter aircraft and three helicopter manufacturers. The indigenous medium transport aircraft is now being deployed in many roles including surveillance and supply dropping. But the biggest leap has been in military electronic systems, specially sensors and process automation ('Command and Control' systems). In fact, India has become a world leader in these technologies, especially in software intensive systems.

Let us now look at the Dashboard as it looks in 2050.

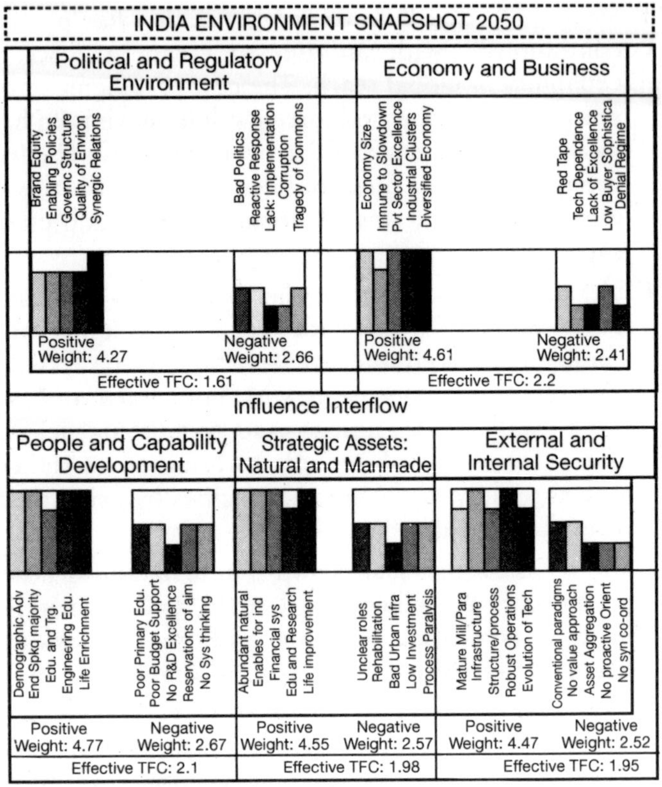


## OBSERVATIONS AND ANALYSIS

One sees all round progress in all strategy areas, and amelioration of negative factors in the broad-based rise of India. The positive weights have increased over decades and are in the value range of 4.27 to 4.77, indicating high level of all round advancement. The negative factors have been ameliorated to a great extent, signifying effective neutralizing the challenges. The effective TFC of around 2 for all strategy areas confirms predominance of constructive over the problematic. The ratio between (i) efforts towards future building v/s (ii) effort for problem resolution, which was almost 50:50 in 2010, has improved towards the desirable Pareto ratio of 80:20. This has spawned a positive feedback loop, wherein the positive factors have consistently built up and negative factors have been diminishing.

Let us now recount substantial changes.

## Political and Regulatory Environment

1. The political strategy areas have seen some serious effort in recasting policies and improving governance processes and structures. It is because of this that India is now considered an easy place to do business in.
2. An area in which the political leadership has achieved commendable success is the global linkage building. Gone are the days when India used to be a laggard in multilateral relation building or being a part of important forums. India is now proactively engaged with all major trade groups and also is a initiator of many dialogues that have major influence on the world affairs. The African Industrial Resurrection Forum (AIRF) has been largely instituted and activated with India and China being the main catalysts.
3. The above two have been made possible by the changed landscape in Indian politics. In place of fragmented, fratricidal and divisive polity, the political thought has consolidated around two parties, the "Sarv Jan Party" with 'left of center' ideology and The "Desh Bhakt Party" with right of center policies. Both the parties have economy and progress as their main plank and aggressively promote their policies as being more progressive than that of the other party.
4. The cleaning of politics has ameliorated many negative factors. Though bad politics still rears its head because of remnants of old political styles, but by and large 'stone walling' responses are gone because the general public no more tolerates innuendoes and chicanery any more. The corruption has been made difficult because there have been exemplary punishment for some in high places (including many cabinet ministers and a tycoon). The power grabbing by the entrenched however

has not been eliminated totally, but there is ascendancy of much more political talent now.

## Economy and Business

5. Economy has been the best facet of India's rise. Not only has India become largest economy of the world, but it has done so without creating any large fissures in India's social system or upsetting the global political applecart. The steady economic growth has been built around the central theme of sustainable development. The Indian industry is not only efficient in usage of natural resources, but also innovative in processes and recyclable materials.
6. The Indian growth has been made possible by the effort of many, and private sector has a huge part in it. The SME segment has come into it's own after 2020. In fact the India has become an innovation driven economy only after proliferation of high tech SME segment. Engineer entrepreneurs have done remarkably well in electronics components, embedded systems, software services (especially web enabled process automation), food processing, mechanical design, UAVs, Surveillance systems and many other fields. There have been great strides in pharmaceutical and health related research by young entrepreneurs, especially in Delhi, Hyderabad and Mysore regions.
7. Indian economy can be called truly broad based now, with low dependence on import of technology. In fact, India is a major exporter of technology in automobiles, electronics, IT services, aviation components, UAVs and pharmaceuticals.
8. The quick growth would not have been possible without major shift in procurement philosophy and policy. The earlier 'One Shot' policy, divorced from long-term technology and system evolution has been totally overhauled and has been a major factor in innovations in high tech areas, especially in UAV technology and 'Process automation' systems. In fact e-governance and

most of the communications and entertainment industry finds technology impetus from local industry now.

## People and Capability Development

9. The Indian demography has become a gold mine for India. Not only has the Indian specialists scripting success stories in India but in all other geographies as well. Free visa regimes with Western countries have allowed Indian engineers and scientists to earn laurels in many fields. Half of the Silicon Valley startups now have Indian connection. Most of the top 100 non-Indian MNCs have subsidiaries in India. Most of the aviation and auto majors have design centers in Bangaluru or Pune.
10. The number of trained workers has been a critical factor in the expansion of size and scope of the Indian industry. The manpower intensive industries specially, e.g. Software development, healthcare, knowledge process outsourcing, education, hospitality and retail has expanded exponentially and each of these cater not only for the burgeoning Indian middle class but a lot of clientele from other countries too. It is estimated that Indian workforce has swelled to 850 million by the year 2050, not counting the rural sector deployment.
11. Qualified high tech workers from India are in demand, especially in Western countries (because of acute shortage of trained manpower) and Middle East (because of higher demand for skills available in India). The number of financial specialists available in financial sector has induced most of the financial organizations to move their high-volume operations to India. Back-office operations have become synonymous with an Indian subsidiary.
12. The education system in India has been overhauled and by 2030, Indian universities were turning out more than a million engineers and for the first time in 2036, there were more than 50,000 doctorates awarded. Many major educational institutions have a campus

somewhere in India (most of the top 20 in the world) and exchange programs are the norm rather than exception.

13. The education institutions are on the forefront of primary research and many industry sponsored programs in IITs and NITs are ubiquitous. In fact research has become a larger part of study curriculum as it sets up a information exchange medium between the students and prospective employers for their deployment in the related industry too.
14. There are many programs that Defense research runs in the top-line engineering colleges to let prospective engineers to work on right in their colleges. It provides colleges domain information and defense research institutions a larger bandwidth for a lot of experimental work that need be done on those technologies.

### Strategic Assets: Natural and Manmade

15. The biggest enabler for industrial and economic development has been the managed urban development in the last 30 years. After being a laggard in investing in urban development till 2020, India has taken this challenge on high priority. From the low investment of (US$ 20 per person per year) in 2010, the investment stands at US$ 220 per person per year. The new cities, specially the industrial cluster hubs have been built on PPP basis and the large capital investment has been permitted a 30 year payback period by letting the local government keep a major portion of revenues generated by the city. It is estimated that US$ 600 billion has been invested by Indian investors and FIIs in the new city projects.
16. Most of the enablers for industry like power, communications, water, civic amenities are now being run as corporate entities. The efficiencies and assurance of these services is now at globally acceptable levels. More than US$ 2 trillion has been invested in assets related to these services, with non-governmental sector

owning more than 50 per cent of these assets. Except for nuclear power stations, private sector has overtaken the government leverage in creation of most classes of these assets.

17. The civic administration of the vibrant new cities is in the hands of local governments that are headed by an elected mayor. A larger proportion of the revenues generated by a city is now invested on maintaining and growing the city rather than being controlled by the state government.
18. Most of the cities now being administered locally have a sense of pride in being more advanced than others. There is a healthy competition between various cities for attracting business as well as cultural excellence. Each city has tried to develop a differentiating competitive advantage for the purpose. Bangalore and Delhi now have the best underground metro rail system. Agra, Jaipur, Jodhpur and Pune have the best maintained historical monuments. Delhi, Mumbai and Chennai have the best maintained airports in Asia. Delhi, Hyderabad, Bangalore and Mumbai compete in providing best shopping experience. The list is endless.
19. The fierce competition and expectation of the general populace is pushing city administration to be pro-active and quick in response. The earlier lethargic officials and lack of action is a thing of past.
20. The life experience enhancement activities are now a star attraction for many cities. The filmdom at Mumbai, Chennai, Hyderabad and Noida are a draw for not only Indian visitor but also for foreign tourists. The music festivals at Jalandhar and Pune attract aficionados from all over the world. The IPL (Indian Premier League) cricket tournament attracts participation from all cricket superstars of the world.
21. The health services, the entertainment centers, education services have reached world class levels.

## External and Internal Security

22. The Indian military services are now a truly professional force with a global mandate. From space to underwater, India has all elements of a potent force that can be flexibly deployed against a variety of challenges of the future.
23. India has taken diplomatic initiatives to maintain peace in her neighborhood. India's borders are quiet. With quick deployment and multi-prong attack capability, India can now undertake any missions anywhere in the world and in space.
24. The military power projection is based on 'state of the art' technology that is being developed in the country by a concerted effort between private sector, Defense Research and Development, Defense PSUs and academia. Thanks to the software prowess early in this century (and most defense systems being software dependent), India has a substantial advantage in innovating new technologies and systems for deployment in Defense. Not surprisingly, UAV and 'Process Automation' is the forte of Indian industry.
25. The police services have become decidedly pro-active and effective after adoption of technology and systems in a major way after 2015. The ground based and airborne video surveillance systems have increased the 'situation awareness' of the force, and mobility on land and air platforms have created a much responsive force. The National Police Information network provides a unified database and a-priori warning system for the police force.
26. The above-said changes in military and police operations would not have been possible without a major mindset change in the uniformed services. That is their changed perception about technology usage. Technology is now considered a major component of operational capability. So, acquiring, deploying, leveraging, optimizing, evolving and superceding technologies and systems is a

part of evolving capabilities. So now asset acquisition (or asset aggregation or hoarding) has been replaced by value capture through technology and systems. The optimization of value by coordination and cooperation, using information sharing and dissemination to maximize advantage, to leverage technological excellence without owning it (outsourcing to a sister organization) are the new methodologies adopted after giving up the silos of influence by many of these organizations. For example, Indian Air Force is the nodal agency for UAV systems and even the police force can seek temporary usage or acquisition through IAF for UAV systems. Similarly Indian Army is the nodal agency for all works services and ground based platforms for all military and paramilitary organizations.

27. Min of Defense is now actively engaged with private industry and academia for research and development of new processes and systems for widespread deployment in services. The technology and systems and road maps are now created by synchronizing technology and 'Military threat' projections.

## Conclusion

### *How Did it Happen: Who Did it*

If we were to seek five most important causal factors that have allowed India to reach the pinnacle of national progress in the short period of 40 years time, there may be a multitude of opinions. Let us give it a try with the proviso that we have to keep revising our thoughts and assessment as India progresses from one stage to another.

So let us try.

1. Prospering of Democracy, Transformation of political thought and environment.
2. Demographic boon.
3. Cyclical civilization changes, Decline of western civilizations and rise of the East. Cultural Inheritance, rich civilization, English speaking populace.

4. Technology dispersion and empowering of India.
5. Amelioration of many constraining social dogmas and removal of 'elephant ropes'.

Some of these (2 and 3) happened due to the forces of nature and time, and some of these were a result of purposeful hard work of millions of individuals (politicians, technologists, researchers, factory workers, educators, government servants, defense men, etc.).

The window of opportunity opened for India and millions put their effort together for making Rise of India possible.

Now on, it requires continued effort for India to stay at the top of their success in the coming future.

# 6

# Monitoring India's Rise: Dismal Scenario 2050

**31 March 2050**

Even after those many years, the voice of the eminent hockey commentator Jasdev Singh still rings in my ears. During the live radiocast of hockey matches, he would follow every move of many a Indian strikers dribbling the ball towards the adversary's goal, his voice steadily increasing to a higher crescendo, and at the end of an unsuccessful assault on the goal, the famous lament,

> "Phir wahi galat nishana, aur Bharat ne ek aur mauka kho diya"
>
> [The wrong aim again, and India has lost yet another opportunity]
>
> Another sport (cricket) and another of his oft-repeated moans,
>
> "Phir off stump ke bahar jaati gend se chhed chhaad aur natija wahi"
>
> [Yet again, messing around with the ball outside the off-stump, with the same disastrous result]

As a dedicated (and sometimes over-emotional) young sports fan, my heart would beat faster and faster till the rebuke would stop the adrenalin and then the heart would sink.

As I have grown in years, I have had 'Jasdev Singh' moments in many other forms and situations. For me, these expressions have assumed larger connotations than just a disastrous sports event. And today's manifestation is weightier as well as dismal.

Today I am deep in thoughts about the state of Indian economy and progress. Just 40 years back, we were the 'toast of the town'; India was considered the rising star. Today we are the proverbial other 'toast', an 'also ran' who nobody is betting on.

Well, in 2010, we made some predictions, that India is going to get to a place of prominence in world affairs in the oncoming half century. That was forty years back and most of those projections have, well, remained projections and never became the big 'step by step' realization of potential, that were the sine qua non of those projections. We kept wasting our energy in innuendoes (fishing outside the off stump) without ever getting to do some serious scoring, and kept losing matches. In the meanwhile, our demographic boon has slowly and steadily turned into a bane. Our inability to improve education, infrastructure and policy framework for industrialization and job creation, has whittled away this God given but one-time blessing. Our biggest asset, the prospective workers have struggled to enroll for education/training, faced low employment prospects and could never get opportunities to graduate to the productivity levels that they were capable of. On the other hand, thanks to the populist politicking, lay people addicted to freebees (though falsely promised and scarcely delivered) have slowly got into the habit of clamoring for more freebees by way of more concessions and higher reservations. Our politicians have turned 'promising without committing' into a fine art, without ever wanting to increase the pie, except when for cutting a big slice for themselves.

Consequently, those 2010 projections seem like a mathematical utopia in 2050. India only flattered to deceive briefly in 2010s with 9 per cent growth initially which petered out when our Neros were playing the flute. The much hyped BRICS group still remains as the major world economic group, but sadly the "I" in the middle of BRICS now stands for Indonesia and not India.

Look at the bars for comparison. The blue bars were the projections made by most of the think tanks and organizations like World Economic Forum and World Bank in 2010. The purple bars were the actual achievement as assessed in 2050. The figures seem to make the progress look so very belabored and incremental. By 2050, India had a potential to become the largest economy, but the actual achievement turned out to be a fraction.

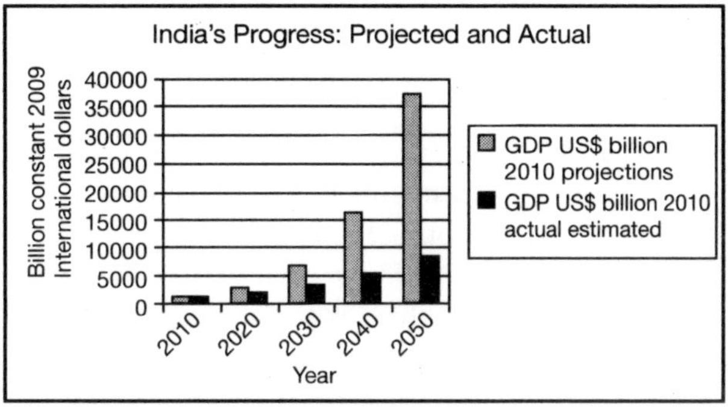


What happened? How did we 'miss the bus' yet again, despite the entire 'How to' advice and precautionary noise that the 'think tanks' were making? Did we take the wrong aim so many times (as Jasdev Singh said many times)? Or did we keep fishing outside the off stump? (Actions that repeatedly brought disaster, but we kept doing these for narrow gains, like not letting go of centralized control). Can we apportion blame? (We do have a lot of experience in our polity for the purpose). Is there a way we can get out of the hole that we have dug for ourselves?

Let us first enumerate the major things that happened or did not happen,

### Political and Regulatory Environment

1. India's GDP, which was projected to grow at 8 per cent+ between 2010 and 2020, spluttered back to Hindu rate of growth of 3.4 per cent by 2017. The reasons were many, but the major stumbling block was the policy paralysis with the Indian political leadership tied up in knots on the (non)issues of reservations (for minorities, religion based, reservations within reservations), regionalism (Maratha pride, sons of soil, language based re-demarcations) and many other

populist policies. We started with India being 1 per cent of the global economy, had set a sight on becoming a quarter or one third of global economy by 2050 (as India was in the seventeenth century), but then we let our narrow parochial interests take over and we are back to being the non-consequential 5.5 per cent of world economy. Meanwhile, China grew from 2 to 35 per cent of global economy.

2. In 2014, the corruption cases involving politicians (US$ 35 billion 2G spectrum case, 13 billion CWG scam, military acquisitions, land grabbing in Mumbai and Delhi, etc.) have became a 'tug of war' between the judiciary and the polity, with the common man looking at it as a mute and bewildered spectator. In fact between 2000 and 2012, scams with a value of US$ 1.8 trillions had been unearthed [http://www.rediff.com/business/slide-show/slide-show-1-the-biggest-scams-in-india/20101230.htm]. The figures thereafter have multiplied many times over. The shenanigans have left no time in the last forty years for the ruling class to bother themselves with the issues that were the real work for India's progress (Industrialization, urban development, enablers).
3. The brand equity of India has taken a big knock in these 40 years. Both investors and other trade blocks have a negative view of 'business environment' because of the restrictive policies and rampant corruption in governance. Transparency International has rated India as 110 out of 120 countries for 'ease of doing business' this year, i.e. 2048. And we have been receiving similar ratings from many agencies for at least twenty years. But nothing gets done because most of the corruption is in high places. The 'high and the mighty' have no qualms about siphoning off the assets as they are able to get around a tardy justice system each time. The rest of the world has found better economies to do business with rather than get into the minefield of Indian governance and bureaucracy.

4. With worldwide oil reserves plummeting as compared to earlier estimates, the oil shock of 2022 has had a deleterious effect on India's growth, a downturn that India never fully recovered from. The balance of payment situation thereafter has been always remained a concern. On the other hand, even with rupee depreciation, exports have not picked up. The fuel rationing in 2030s have further decelerated the growth of automobile and aviation industries. The aggregate effect has been FE reserves plummeting down to a few billion dollars and it is becoming difficult for India to maintain liquidity for her essential requirements even.
5. India's exclusion from the BRICS and economic slowdown after 2035 has constrained the development strategy of India. The investment in urban infrastructure scaling and improvement has reduced to a trickle. Meanwhile, the persistent urban migration has resulted in proliferation of slums and hence lower quality of life in the cities. The slum population in large cities that had come down from 25 per cent in 2010 to 12 per cent in 2020 has climbed yet again to 20 per cent in 2045. But this time, the number base is different. Out of the one billion urban dwellers, 200 million stay in slums now, a figure 10 times the 2010 slum dweller statistics.
6. Indian politics remains under the stranglehold of entrenched interest. The dynastic roll-overs are in third and fourth generation. The rest of the political space is occupied by the rich and unscrupulous. The democratic exercise has lost relevance because formation of the government at the center or in states is an exercise in horse-trading rather than setting the political mandate for the next government. When the election promises are not kept, the voters keep rejecting the incumbents in the hope that the new dispensation will be progressive and forward looking. But election after election, it is the same old wine in new bottles. The parties and elected MPs change allegiance and the final shape of the government and their policies bear no resemblance

to the enunciated poll promises. Year after year, ministerial berths are traded as bargaining chips and the new ministers have no track record for proficiency in that function. Consequently, governance has gone steadily downhill.

7. Divisive politics has created a chasm between center and state governments. It has become almost impossible to get any consensus on any major policy initiative between all states and central government. The co-ordination for even critical activities such as taxation, infrastructure planning and build, anti-terrorism measures and disaster management has become impossible. There is a perpetual war of words between various governing entities, especially if the state government is from another political group.
8. There is no party with all-India footprint anymore. The regional parties align with one major political party or the other in lieu of the goodies offered. Each of these regional parties holds a virtual veto power over the ruling party, so no tough decisions can be taken. In addition, the regional parties feel free to destabilize the incumbent government on whims and fancy; and bring another party to power. This has created a paradox in Indian democracy. Major parties have a lot of responsibility and limited political leverage. Smaller (even a single member) parties have a lot of leverage (power) but no responsibility. These shenanigans have become the essence of politics. Hence next to no attention on the planning and progress of the nation in the last thirty years.
9. The bureaucracy has, in this environment of fratricidal politics, adopted a safe though destructive (for the nation) policy. With each new dispensation of government, they cannot be seen as being too close to the previous incumbents. So they have perfected the art of maintaining equal distance from all political combinations. Unfortunately, it also results in keeping a distance from efficient and progressive administration.

As a result, the bureaucracy has adopted upward compatibility, amorphous interface with citizens and 'keeping my tail clear' kind of approach. The citizens in India get nothing back as benefits from the government machinery in return for being honest tax payers.

10. The real-estate and other assets (mines, agricultural land, buildings, ports, airports, information hubs, and financial assets) have been cornered by an elite minority and the well entrenched cartels decide the cost of most products and services in India. The monopolies, duopolies and cartels do not allow fair competition and Indian consumers have to pay a higher price for everything that they need and consume.

## Economy and Business

11. India became the third largest economy in 2011 on Purchase Power Parity basis and was expected to become the second largest economy of the world in the year 2039. That required a growth rate of 8-9 per cent for the period 2020-40. But the restrictive policies and regressive politics got in the way and India dropped down to Hindu rate of growth in 2017 itself. We let the BRICS overtake us one by one. Now in the year 2050, we have slid down in size as a percentage of global economy (5.5 per cent) and are facing a danger of losing our sixth position to some of the new BRICS. The current rate of <3 per cent growth is going to weaken our position even more until we can come up with revolutionary new policies.
12. India's initial economic growth was robust because it was balanced, dependent on exports (30 per cent) but more on domestic consumption (70 per cent). The burgeoning middle class was the anchor of growth. As middle class grew more prosperous, it further created a market for further economic output. But as growth slowed, so did the growth of income for the middle class. The ensuing effect has been a negative spiral, both for middle class and for economic growth. The

consumption grew anemically in 2040s and has started contracting in 2047. Soon, an economic depression may well be in the offing.

13. Private sector growth in India has reached a plateau and there has been a perceptible move by Indian MNCs to move out to more business friendly locations in South America and East Asia. The first time the outward investment exceeded inward investment was in 2027. Thereafter it has been continuous flight of capital from the country. Currently, US$ 10 billion on the average are being invested abroad by Indian private sector despite restrictions on outflows. Not surprisingly, India's FE reserves are at all time low in 2050.
14. Some of the new industrial towns wear a deserted look. The auto ancillary and steel industry is the hardest hit. The new mega city, 'Ispatnagar' in Bihar has become a welfare case requiring large scale humanitarian effort for rehabilitation of laid off workers because of large scale closure of steel industry.
15. The vibrant economy in 2010s had spawned the expansion of retail, entertainment, health, education and many other industries. These domains after growing till 2030 have fallen on bad times. The higher professional education and specialist training organizations have been particularly hit hard. Starting 2030, many of the education clusters have evolved to offering new services.
16. Indian defense industry is steadily facing contraction and closure. The large investment that Indian MNCs made in new product development especially in UAVs, Information systems and other 'Command and Control' systems, have induced no new system acquisitions from defense and other ministries. The export market is too tough for Indian MNCs to penetrate.
17. India became the target of disinvestments by FIIs, firstly in 2030s, when the Indian rupee was depreciated and the large stake of the FIIs lost dollar value by

25 per cent in a few months. Thereafter the outflow has accompanied every downturn of the stock market.

18. The Industrial clusters in Bangalore, Noida, Gurgaon, Pune, new Hyderabad, Coimbatore and Indore have been facing increasing deterioration of infrastructure and businesses have been moving to other 2nd tier cities, and in 2030s, alarmingly, to other locations in Asia.

19. The aviation industry, which had some minor problems in mid 2010s, has faced life threatening squeeze of higher costs and declining market all through 2030s and 2040s. There has been closure of two major airlines including the state airline that had been provided bailouts almost every year for 20 years. The crumbling airport systems, inefficient Air Traffic Control has made air travel an inefficient and a costly mode of transportation, hurting the bottom line of airlines business. The large investment of airlines in large fleets in 2030s and 2040s has put a further strain on the airlines. If some momentous decisions are not taken soon, we will certainly see closure of the remaining airlines.

## People and Capability Development

20. During 2010s and 2020s, there was an expectation of a renaissance in engineering education. Given the latency of the talent development and the premise that demographic advantage is the biggest differentiating factor for Indian progress, major investment and policy push was being bandied about in all quarters in 2010s. But beyond talk shows, it was only incremental approach and lack of investment. The half hearted approach put paid to this cardinal requirement. Not only budgetary support was always insufficient, the government policy stymied the private players' effort also. The private educational institutions were considered at par with any other source of tax revenues rather than participants of a strategic initiative and have been exposed to the

same regime of permits and permissions. In addition to our failure to scale education and training, India has fallen back on quality of education, too. The IITs that were considered the bootstrap for creating world class engineering education (and academic research) have stagnated and the new IITs have not been established due to lack of investment. The foreign universities, who were keen to set up Indian campuses, have lost interest and found better alternatives in Singapore, China and Malaysia.

21. The primary education coverage remained poor even after special initiatives were undertaken in 2013 and 2027. The investment remained less than 4 per cent of GDP (though it was recommended to be hiked to 6 per cent of GDP by many studies and commissions). But more importantly, the implementation remained another instrument of siphoning off funds from the government kitty by the unscrupulous field officials. In 2050, we are better than only some backward African countries in enrollment and dropout rates. The enrollment of girls even in 2050 remains below 60 per cent.
22. R&D remains the last priority of the educated class and the government. After being ahead of China till 2020, India pales in comparison today in patents and basic research. In private sector, the new product development is on hold in a shrinking market, making R&D effort even poorer. As a share of GDP, in 2049, India spent one per cent on R&D as compared to 3.5 per cent in China, Considering that China is now seven times bigger economy, the R&D effort in India is miniscule, thus leaving no opportunities for catch up in science and technology.
23. The education system and governance are now showing the repercussions of using reservations as a political tool. India's overall capability repertoire is lesser than it would have been in a competitive environment. In competition with China, it is a

huge disadvantage, because, as we had intended, we cannot counter their quantitative advantage with our qualitative advantage.

24. The growing unemployment of the young people (especially in the urban slums) has become a festering law and order problem. After 2026, when the sudden slowdown caused the unemployment rate to shoot above 5 per cent (not counting the rural unemployment or under employment), we recovered to a rate of 3.5 per cent for a while in 2030s, but after the slowdown, 6 per cent is supposed to be a manageable rate. Considering the 60 million workers on the roads, the demographic boon has become a demographic disaster. We haven't seen the worst yet.
25. The abandoned old people and children are becoming a social problem, especially in urban slums. The problem is likely to assume monstrous proportions in the next 10 years, when the people born by the turn of the century start retiring.

### Strategic Assets: Natural and Manmade

26. 'Integrated urban planning and uplift' Law, 2018, that made it mandatory for all state governments to follow the basic guidelines of sustainable growth and quality of life assurance, has been largely ignored by the state governments because of political posturing. There has been a clear intention to retain centralized control of finances in respect of urban administration by state governments of all hues despite the crumbling infrastructure and the threat of business moving away. The devolution of powers to city corporations under this law has been ignored till the deterioration in the infrastructure has earned us the sobriquet of the 'nation with the dirtiest cities'. What else can be expected if eight out of the ten most polluted and dirtiest cities of the world are in India?
27. The investment in urban development, which was the lowest to begin with (in 2010s it was one sixth of China

and one twentieth of western cities) saw an upward trend briefly in 2020s, and then stagnated at those levels. The city revenues were usurped by state governments for diversion to populist by unproductive schemes (e.g., Rozgar Yojana, Food Security Program, Health Assurance Plan, etc.). All these schemes achieved little but were good poll planks for many political satraps. Consequently, urban infrastructure that was starved of investment is at a breakpoint.

28. Public Private Partnership that was mooted for bringing in the much required investments in urban development never took off because of the restrictive policy framework. On top of that the influence peddling reserved the top industrial cities for the well-connected. The cities have been left to fend for themselves on shoe-string budgets.
29. The enablers, e.g. Power, communication, transportation, health services and conservancy services are in bad shape because of the same reasons, i.e. low investments and restrictive policies for private players.
30. Our rivers are dying thanks to overexploitation for drinking water, agriculture and industry. The various initiatives like 'Clean Ganga Campaign' and 'Save Narmada Andolan' have been feeble attempts, but in view of no administrative and financial support, these initiatives have petered out to forgotten efforts.
31. The Indian landscape in general is now seen as chaos and filth ridden. The tourists flow has dried up even at old-time favorite destinations like Agra, Rajasthan, Karnataka, Goa. There were only 2.2 million tourists in 2048, an all time low in the last fifty years.

### External and Internal Security

32. Since 2010, the perspective plan envisaged US$ 100 billion acquisitions for Defense modernization in the period 2010-20. It took India six years to get its

aircraft procured through the MMRCA proposal on its runways. Even thereafter, the procurements have been marred by delays, 'one by one' purchases (not a graded induction as per a long-term force capability plan), without synchronous development of local industry, and sans technology absorption. So we remain addicted to technology and systems imports and that has been a big drain on our FE reserves.

33. Lack of top down approach and 'one shot inductions' has limited us to remain a defensive force, with fragmented capabilities in certain areas. Our neighbors, meanwhile, have gone from defensive to regional, and onwards to global capabilities. So all our preparations have still not created the secure environment for sustained economic growth and peaceful social life. Even our Western neighbor has stolen a march over us in UAVs. We run the risk of a disadvantage not only in a conventional war situation but also face constant needling in a low intensity war. We have seen increase in low-level intrusions by UAVs over the years.

34. India's borders and boundaries are now being increasingly violated by aggressive neighbors, because of gaps in technology deployment and because adversaries know that India does not have the military and economic potential to fight a war against a much superior neighbor.

35. Private sector is now effectively disengaged from defense and homeland security domains. As local procurement dry up (due to import addiction and also because of tortuous procurement procedures) there is effectively no economic rationale for the private sector to invest and develop systems. The industry/academia linkage on high technology projects is also dysfunctional.

Let us now look at the Dashboard as it looks in 2050.

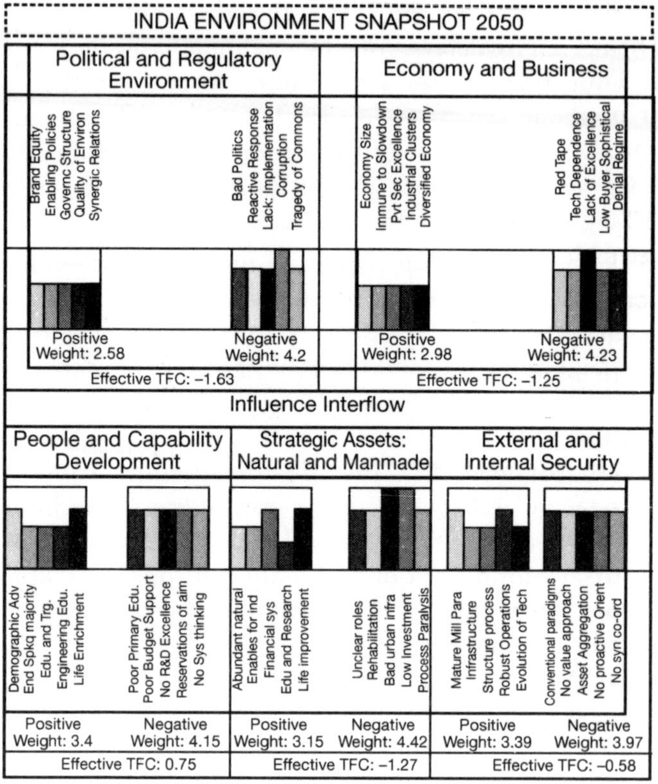


## OBSERVATIONS AND ANALYSIS

One sees slow withering away of positive factors in all strategy areas, the values coming down from 4+ to 3 in the intervening 40 years. That means that the effort for constructive development has gradually been reducing. The reason is there to see in the value of the negative factors that have snowballed to major problems during this decline of India. More and more of effort and resources are being diverted to resolving problems rather than productive investment towards future growth. The ratio between (i) efforts towards future building v/s (ii) effort for problem resolution, which was almost 50:50 in 2010, is tending towards the dreaded reverse Pareto ratio of 20:80. This has spawned a negative feedback loop, wherein the negative factors have assumed dangerous proportions and positive factors have been fading.

The negative factors outgun the positive ones in all strategy areas. Thus India stands submerged in negative spiral of ever bigger problems and lesser progressive changes. Compared to BRICS, the prognosis becomes even starker. India stagnates while other nations gallop away to new heights in economic, military and soft power prowess.

Let us look at the some significant aspects of the situation.

### Political and Regulatory Environment

1. The political strategy areas have seen gradual eroding of the advantage of India's democratic tradition. The divisive and exploitative politics has not only continued but has developed some forms that have damaged the very foundations of democracy in India. Firstly, the religion and caste are now major determinants in elections and a large political space has been now ceded to religious leaders. These religious heads have no priority or taste for matters of economy or industry, but for preserving their turf. Second is the perpetuation of dynastic succession at every level. We have third or fourth generation of political families, peddling the same old thoughts and philosophies. The new policy push or initiatives are conspicuous by their absence from the scene for decades now.
2. The rest of the world has lost interest in India. India, a beacon of democratic thought, excellence in IT and with a large pool of English speaking workforce was the envy of the world. Now in 2050, with the democratic tradition more of a lost dream, IT excellence lost to BRICS and developing African countries, and a semi-skilled workforce (60 million unemployed and another 100 million underemployed because of lack of hands-on skills) induces no envy but avoidance. No rising powers are keen on building any trade relationships and partnerships because of policy and governance deficit.

3. The entrenched politics has hijacked the political process in a way that the voters have choice between one entrenched group or another of the same kind. The entry of erudite and professionally qualified in politics has been constrained because of undeserving defending their turf with all means, fair and foul.
4. The governance, the institutions, the policy framework and the political thought have not evolved with times. Till the political environment becomes progressive, governance and the brand equity of India as a democratic progressive nation is restored, we will not be able to compete and prosper as a nation.

### Economy and Business

5. Economy would have been the best facet of India's rise. From third largest in 2010, to the topmost or thereabouts in 2050, that was the expectation. What could have been US$ 88 trillion or may be 100, has crumbled down to single figures. What India did not spend on education, urban renewal, industrial and technology assets, has been and is being spent on law enforcement, flood and disaster relief and subsidies for the poor and suffering. Despite having abundance of resources, natural and human, we have squandered all advantage in mismanagement.
6. The socialistic pattern of society in earlier times and dynastic (status quo) politics in 2010s and thereafter, has underwritten disproportionate investment in PSUs and government sector (for maintaining control). The private sector, especially the SMEs, who were expected to make a substantial contribution in industrial growth, found it difficult to prosper because of this policy bias. In US, SMEs contribute 30 per cent to the economy and in China the figure is a phenomenal 60 per cent. In India, after rising to a figure of 22 per cent in 2012, the SMEs have found it difficult to maintain growth and the figure stagnated at about 20 per cent. Another reason for stunted growth of SME segment was that

government steadfastly refused to procure high tech systems from SMEs and limited them to being suppliers of sundries. Thus in big government expenditure categories, e.g. Defense, Infrastructure, e-governance, where SMEs could have been innovators, technology developers and managed service providers, SMEs have been kept out by policy.

7. The diversification of Indian economy into new products and services has not been sustained after 2020 because of slowdown in growth, and also because of private sector losing motivation for R&D.

### People and Capability Development

8. The Indian demography has become a bane rather than a boon because we have not harnessed this God given gift by creating the enablers. Education remains a neglected field and political class has shown more interest in job reservations than in job creation.
9. The semi-skilled workers now form a large proportion of the workforce. In some regions (like the states in Gangetic plains) unemployable outnumber the skilled and employable workers. The social institutions are under strain to support 60 million unemployed and 100 million underemployed.
10. Because of the economic conditions, Indians are not able to secure opportunities in other countries also. The employability of young Indians is now becoming a major issue.
11. The primary education system in India, because of lack of investments, has been bursting at the seams. After 2035, the system has worked over its capacity. Though number of new enrollments has declined in 2040, but the quality remains sub-optimal. The dropout rate is high and the girl enrollment still trails that of boys' enrollment.
12. The education institutions primary research programs remain under-funded. Industry sponsored research has almost vanished from IITs and other institutions.

**Strategic Assets: Natural and Manmade**

13. That demographic advantage is going to underwrite India's rise, has been known since 2010. We also knew that it entailed that we will do many things (urban infra, education and training, clustering, etc.) for harnessing this advantage. The most important action point was the urban development; to provide these new workers with living space, civic amenities, life improvement opportunities for them and their families. It was expected that as our work-age population increases steadily, and more of them move to urban (industrial) clusters, our urban areas will develop in synchronism. The planned and sustained investment for the purpose was the cornerstone of the industrial expansion in the planned cluster. But it did not happen. The lack of political wisdom (and urban planning despite the dedicated ministry), the fratricidal fight (between central and state governments) for financial control and failure to devolve administrative powers to local bodies (from state governments to city councils) have resulted in status quo rather than the quick growth that was required. From the investment level of US$ 20 per person per year in 2010 (which was one of the lowest in by other BRICS), the investment increased only incrementally to US$ 65 per person per year in 2030. Most of this investment was used up in removing fault lines rather than scaling. Unlike China, we have no new mega cities. The PPP model has never taken off and we have not been able to create urban infrastructure, required for the projected progress.
14. Most of the enablers for industry like power, communications, water and civic amenities are plagued by shortages of capacity and inefficiencies, even in 2050, despite ambitious plans about nuclear energy, hydro schemes and privatization of many services. The staggered investment of US$ 2 trillion was bandied about, but successive governments withdrew the financial support to many projects mid-way, throwing

all plans and investments in disarray. These plans and schemes have proved to be ad-hoc and no long-term road map has been followed through. There are no assured service levels even in 2050. Not a conducive situation for industrial growth that was envisaged.

15. The local city administration is still run in remote control mode from the state headquarters. The local elected officials have no powers and government departments run by the diktats of bureaucracy in the state capitals. The cities are crumbling rather than growing.
16. The health services and education services have deteriorated to a low level, but for a few bright spots in the private sector. The only industry that has kept its head high is the entertainment industry. But this is purely private sector effort and it is also because of Indian audiences' addiction to 'song and dance' (and also cricket).

### External and Internal Security

17. The Indian military services have not been able to keep up with the evolving challenges. Be it the adversaries on the northern borders, terrorists infiltrating from the seas, by air or through barbed wire fences. Our supply sea-lanes are under threat form the aggressive new military powers and we are not able to respond to our adversaries' parries and thrusts.
18. India has not seized much of diplomatic initiatives to maintain peace in her neighborhood. In fact the adversaries are now joined in their inimical designs against India.
19. Our military capability lacks 'state of the art' technology base. Our adversaries have stolen a march over us by investing much more in R&D. We are now being constantly threatened and tested by new weapon systems like UAV, space based sensors and directed energy weapons, while we still have not come out of import addiction. Our domestic military industry remains in

doldrums, thanks to our procurement policies that prefers established MNCs.

20. The police services remain corruption ridden and under the thumb of polity. The urban centers (especially the industrial centers with declining industry and unemployment) have become hotbeds of Mafiosi and goondas. The police cannot do anything but be a mute spectator to the mayhem and destruction of public/ private property, when the mobs go out of control. The mafia and terrorists have found a common interest in keeping things on the boil, and it is becoming difficult to distinguish between the terrorists and local ruffians, making law and order an intractable problem.
21. The technology like video surveillance systems has been deployed only in VVIP areas, leaving most of the urban areas vulnerable. The policing or homeland security is reactive and responds to events rather than pro-actively trying to prevent the events.
22. The overarching problem is that military and police organizations have not been able to get rid of the old mindset of manpower intensive operations. The use of processes and technology is still a prop and not mainstream strategy. Also technology acquisition is an afterthought (e.g. we cannot conduct surveillance in a marshy area without a UAV), rather than driven by technology evolution.
23. We missed a golden opportunity to co-opt private sector in Defense system development and production in 2010s. Nor did we harness the latent capabilities of academia for research and development of new processes and systems for deployment in services. The result is that we are addicted to import of technology and systems, and have to make do with de-rated technology that others are willing to part with. That keeps us second to others for all times to come. And we have killed our last refuge (the Indian defense industry) for many years to come.

## Conclusion

### *How Did it Happen: Who Did it*

If we were to seek five most important causal factors that have stopped India from reaching the pinnacle of progress in 2050 (as envisaged in 2010), there are many. But let us look at the important ones.

1. Destabilization of Democracy, deterioration of political thought and environment.
2. Demographic boon turning to bane.
3. 'Status quo' thinking, private sector emasculation, imports addiction.
4. Technology bankruptcy and R&D deprivation.
5. Perpetuation of the social ills and retrograde practices in the name of cultural or civilization superiority.

The best window of opportunity opened for India in 2010s and we did not rise to the occasion. Our Nero (leaders) played the fiddle as the time slipped by. And now we are an 'also ran'; forever ruing 'missing the bus' and trying to handle the obnoxious mix of our slowing economy and graying population.

It requires Herculean effort for India to avoid sliding down in economy, brand equity or quality of life for her citizens.

# 7

# Monitoring India's Rise: Possibilities 2050

## Thinking about Possibilities on 31 March 2050

So now we know what the best possibility (Happy Scenario 2050) is and the worst case prognosis (Dismal Scenario 2050).

What will happen? Will it be either, or something in between?

Let us get real now. The two scenarios mentioned and analyzed in the previous two chapters are extremities and have a very low probability of occurring. The more plausible outcomes are somewhere in-between the two extremes. Let us find out why.

Let us recall the two concepts that we touched upon earlier. The concepts are 'Normal Distribution' and 'Black Swans'. The first one suggests that all things natural are a mixed bag. The second one tells us that exceptional events are more normal in the history of mankind than we would like to believe.

How does 'Normal distribution' help in our finding the plausible scenario? Well, in best scenario, we assume all is good, all politicians are forward looking, all academic institutions scaling and improving, peace and progress prevails all around. In the second, the assumption is all bad; all politicians corrupt, infrastructure crumbling and no respite anywhere. The first one is daydreaming, the other a doomsday prophecy. It is quite like the digital 1 and 0, Yes or No. But in actual life, things are not such clear cut black and white, but many shades of gray. For example, some politicians are exceptional, some outright atrocious and the majority are somewhat good. The normal distribution is representative of this aggregate characteristic of politicians. What varies between one set of politicians (say Happy Scenario) and another (say Dismal scenario) is that the average of their goodness (a positive factor) maybe higher in the first and average of corruption (a negative factor) may be higher in the second. The same law of distribution may apply to the quality (or quantum) of all factors and sub-factors in our earlier discussions.

So if the values are not digital (1 or 0) but stochastic (distributed around a mean), our results are also likely to be similar (stochastic). But once again, we reiterate our intent to keep things simple. So we adopt a simplified schema, a Fuzzy set theoretic representation where we say that outcomes are (say) seven possible values, as follows:

Value 1 = 100 per cent Happy Scenario 2050

Value 2 = 90 per cent Happy Scenario 2050 + 10 per cent Dismal Scenario

Value 3 = 70 per cent Happy Scenario 2050 + 30 per cent Dismal Scenario

Value 4 = 50 per cent Happy Scenario 2050 + 50 per cent Dismal Scenario

Value 5 = 30 per cent Happy Scenario 2050 + 70 per cent Dismal Scenario

Value 6 = 10 per cent Happy Scenario 2050 + 90 per cent Dismal Scenario

Value 7 = 100 per cent Dismal Scenario

So our possibility set is now; India Progress (Value 1, Value 2, ..., Value 7)

We know that Value 1 and Value 7 are extremes and improbable. These are useful to be thought of as bounds (limits) of the set (possibilities).

Let us now get out of the maths and get on with the thinking. The name of the game is to get as close to Value 1 in 2050. (In other words achieve as closely as possible the Happy Scenario 2050.)

But let us make our inference more robust by making use of 'Black Swan' concept too. As there is always uncertainty lurking around the corner (Nassim Nicholas Taleb, *Fooled by Randomness*, Penguin Books 2007, p. viii), we don't know how much will we be buffeted by factors beyond our control or even beyond our frame of thought. But we aim to get as close to Value 1 as possible, and learn to temper our expectations as per the flow of events in future.

Equally important is our effort to avoid going in the other direction, i.e. to counteract the factors that will take us to/towards Value 7.

Push and pull between positive and negative factor will determine the equilibrium state and where we are in the fuzzy set at various epochs in time.

Another precaution is in order here. Trying to oversimplify a complex issue is tantamount to trivializing it. At the same time, we don't want to get drowned in detail. So sticking to our objective that we want to create a helicopter view, we indicate the major areas that should capture India's attention in the years/decades to come, but not talk about prescriptive specific measures that would be the outcome of an elaborate and extensive analysis and planning process.

So let us begin to find the most plausible scenario for India.

We already know the strategy areas, and their factors and sub-factors, whose value will determine India's achievements in future. We need to work in each of those areas for maximizing (minimizing in case of negative factors or sub-factors) values towards the maximal aggregate. We will require specific actions on specific activities and artifacts for the purpose.

There are some patterns and basic axioms that apply in general to every of those actions. These can also be thought of as guiding principles of our planning and implementation actions towards India's growth.

There are two kinds of patterns.

The first pattern of activities (or intellectual predilection) is the kind that if adhered to, will assist India in getting as close to the 'Happy Scenario 2050' as possible (thanks to the uncertainty that the future will throw at us). Let us call these as "Real issues".

The second category of activities and tendencies are the patterns that do not help in progressing towards "Happy Scenario 2025". If anything, these may take India towards "Dismal Scenario 2050" by wasting effort and resources or vitiating the environment so that the positive factors are stunted and negative factors proliferate. We call these "Non-Issues".

Why would someone endorse "Non-Issues". The answer is that not everyone is seized with the love of justice, democracy and social progress (especially if being partial to non-issues results in personal opulence). So there will always be crooks and exploiters to ensure that their gains are assured, without a thought about the larger good of the society or the nation.

It is when the vast majority (and the leadership) of a nation embrace the real issues, that the nation progresses towards the happy scenarios. The converse is true too. If the vast majority (and leadership) gets too busy with non-issues, the dismal scenario cannot be very far away.

So whether India 2050 has Value 1, Value 2...or Value 7, will depend upon how issues and non-issues juxtapose in the years till 2050.

So, it is imperative, that the real issues are given our assent and commitment; and non-issues are repudiated and kept away from sapping our will, energy and time. Let us have a look at the representative list.

### Positive Patterns: Real Issues

1. **Openness:** A substantive issue with considerable connotations. We need to lift the veil of secrecy over all matters official; because the closeted governance is becoming an alibi for inefficiency and waste. We require openness in our planning, implementation, governance and regulatory systems and practices. This is easier said than done because openness need be effectuated at multiple levels; and at present there is more opaqueness than openness at each level. At the highest level, the political leadership has to begin enunciating their five year targets after each election

and declare their scorecard each year. At mid-level, the ministries and departments should have measurable goals and at field level, 'citizen charter' could provide a measure of expected performance from the government machinery. Openness and public awareness will breed commitment and higher performance.

2. **Winning habit and not gloating over a few wins:** What matters is the overall aggregate and not flashes of genius among a multitude of ordinary. Any great effort is a sum total of many individual parts contributing towards overall value, rather than a few making gigantic push while others watch on the sidelines waiting for their share of the fruit of endeavor getting distributed. A simplistic example of aggregate effort is many cylinders of an automobile engine putting out equal power to the crank shaft at an appropriate time to provide good overall performance. We need many more million Indians contributing and not many more Indians waiting for a giveaway.
3. **Proliferation of excellence:** You don't become a super power on by the effort of a few super stars in a few fields. If we are all waiting for a few charismatic leaders and performers, who will pull the whole nation to the lofty greatness, well the wait could be rather long if not never-ending. Taking a cue from America's growth, wide-spread excellence in almost all the fields of endeavor is a 'sine qua non' for a nation's rise to greatness. In case of India, it will have to be many million great performances, year after year, in agriculture, manufacturing, software, aviation, defense, communications, healthcare and many other fields. And biggest of them all, excellence in statesmanship.
4. **Best of breed:** There is nothing like national standards. *You have to excel at global level.* You fly in international environment. You educate in competition with global centers of excellence. You sell, buy, manufacture in collaboration with global entities. No point aiming at

any standards lower than global. Anybody seeking or giving *concessions* is sabotaging India's long-term future.

5. **Persons are not important, roles are:** If you have ever wondered, why a US president is always addressed as Mr. President or why a prime minister or minister in India are called by assignment. The person behind the role is not as important as the role itself. Persons can change, fall sick, be scared, fail or retire; the role doesn't. The biggest mistake for the general public is when they confuse the two with each other. As long as the persons keep trying to fit the role, things remain on even keel. But when the role is fitted to a person, the problems start. We have to get hero (person) worship out of our collective psyche and get the people to perform their roles.
6. **From "Good" to "Good Enough":** Most of us have not chased the moving goalpost of global excellence as yet. And whatever has been considered nice, good and acceptable may be short of being considered 'good enough' for global excellence. And that may also change with growth, i.e. you may have to aim higher and higher to keep setting new standards. This will require an attitudinal change across the scenario, in industry, governance and most importantly in the minds of people.
7. **Strategic thinking and not reactive discourse on minor issues:** Motivated by Pareto principle here, more mind space should be occupied with matters of import (and future growth) and lesser on time-wasters (and follies and fights of the past) that are the result of ego clashes, (perceived or real) inconveniences and dogmas. Prioritization in favor of the more important is the key for keeping focus.
8. **Proportions and not Absolutes:** In human affairs, it is never pure Black or White; there are numerous shades of gray in between. It is always a matter of proportions and more importantly getting the proportions better and better all the time. For example, there would

*always be poor people, but the magic is in pulling increasing numbers out of poverty, rather than promising the utopia of* 'Ram Rajya'. Higher percentage of educated workers, lesser proportion of health problems, infant mortality, school dropouts, higher percentage of performers and superstars...and so on, is the name of the game. We need to banish the extreme and one-sided promises, ideologies, policies and actions and embrace the rational, balanced, incremental and consistent.

9. **Collaborative and not antagonistic:** A nation can become great only with the collaboration of all the members of the society and not if they are always fighting with each other. If the polity is always undoing what the incumbents did before election, the nation will keep undoing the previous five years work rather than building the future.
10. **Harmonization between creation and fulfillment:** The acquisition of life needs have two major aspects, production and distribution. Perfect production but bad distribution results in wasted production. Perfect distribution but sub-optimal production means you waste the distribution channel and create perpetual shortages. Be it services (electricity, sewage, etc.) or foodstuff, both production and distribution have to be matched to get the optimum usage. We need to create means of both creation and delivery to utilize the produce.
11. **Simplism to logical thinking:** We live in times where we are being bombarded with information of all kind. But most of us are so lazy that we do not process that information even for our own good. It is more convenient for us to believe in stereotypes and half truths couched in simplistic but very attractive packaging. We have cricketers advise us on tonics and hairstyling, film stars about car technology, and polity on who to give unbridled power to. Each of these categories, of course, make tons of money giving this advice and has not much of professional training to tell

you about products they advertise. Indians need to give up being gullible; and shift to logical thinking to find out the real intents and act per their own wisdom rather than someone's propaganda.

12. **No to pure entitlement regime:** Herald in a "Balanced Entitlement/Obligation regime": We have been fed so many a spiels about our entitlements (including fundamental rights, assured by our constitution) that we don't even notice that entitlements have bounds and associated obligations. The result is that we land up violating others' rights or cause conflicts/road blocks. Conflicts constrain the aggregation of effort and progress of the nation.
13. **Bring experts to fore:** For the best performance, we need the accomplished people to do the job they do the best. And we need proliferation of this principle. Going to the best doctor for medical advice, best engineer for technology development, best domain expert for development planning, best economist for financial planning, and best scientist for research seems so intuitive. But "Tragedy of the Commons" is always lurking in the background. People trying to get the positions they do not deserve. A nation can progress on the shoulders of the most capable, and not with a preponderance of greed and ineptness.
14. **Dismantle the unnecessary restraining walls:** Constitution provides for equal opportunities. However that has been distorted to mean reservations for the disadvantaged and then this reservation right has been hijacked by the non-deserving. The ensuing complexity of who can/cannot occupy a role has become the cardinal reason for organizations becoming ineffective and inefficient. We need to change over to an open system for talent acquisition for bringing the efficacy and efficiency to the level of an advanced nation while ensuring that the disadvantaged get a level playing field.

15. **Continued excellence and gathering pace:** A developing economy may have "Start and Stops" initially, but as it matures to an advance economy, it develops a 'Continuous momentum'. The environment of a nation should provide continuity and maintenance of direction of progress (no deviations with change in governments or other changes in circumstances).
16. **Proactive tackling of emerging fault lines:** As a nation progresses, new fault lines develop. Envy of competitors, building up of inequities, 'Attractiveness' of stealing readymade luxuries, or plain sadism of destroying things beautiful. We need to develop "environment assurance" capabilities in synchronism.
17. **Defense Preparedness:** Changing from a defensive to a global force: Change over from an asset collection to a process driven approach.

## Negative Patterns: The Non-Issues

1. **Mcguffins:** (*A term used in context of 'film making' and popularized by Alfred Hitchcock. Mcguffins are something ambiguous, undefined, generic, left open to interpretation or otherwise completely unimportant that, in a film, the protagonists are after, but the audience doesn't care.*) Taking a cue from the concept, if the leaders/politicos are the protagonist and the general public the audience, there seem to be numerous Mcguffins that they seem to be after, that have no relevance to public but that keeps the politicos looking hard at work. As if they are doing something very important. For example, the numerous welfare schemes that never benefit Indians (except politicians and bureaucracy), building temples, saving Indian culture, removing poverty (the poverty seems to be hiding where they never find it), etc. The need is to be aware of Mcguffins, not letting politicians *use these to misguide the gullible*, and bringing the discourse back to progress and growth.

2. **The "Tragedy of Commons":** When people share a common resource, those who take the most, gain the most. But everybody suffers the consequence of the resource's decline. But the best employment of common resources is wider dispersion so that a large proportion of public can exploit it and create a large value aggregate.
3. **Caste system:** Need to obliterate unnecessary castes and classes used for 'divide and rule' politics. It is of no consequence if the computer language code is written by a Dalit or Brahmin or Sikh. All that is needed is that it should work well without crashing. Do you really care, who manages your electrical supply or conducts your surgery or operates your bank teller, as long as the service is performed efficiently.
4. **Slavery to generational trends:** What our parents or forefathers were. If my grandfather was a lowly peon, does that condemn me to remain at that level? Or if my great grandfather was a renowned surgeon, does that bestow upon me the right to wield the axe on any unsuspecting patient. Why should a politician's son/daughter be only a politician? Or a businessman's progeny the next tycoon? This inbreeding constrains fresh thinking and innovative action. What matters is what one can do today. The *right to develop to the limit of one's ability* is what matters.
5. **Subservience to history, culture, social mores:** It is nice to be born in a nation with a history, culture and social practices to be proud of. But none of these are stationary and are continuously evolving with time. The road to future is paved with new kinds of human experience, knowledge and of course next generation technology. The past only provides the context in which newness develops. Always harking back to past (only arranged marriages, limiting females in education and professional progress) generally negates the forward evolution. Too many references to past could be a ploy by 'status quo' practicians to cover up their inability to handle the future.

6. **Inheritance of follies and faults:** Inheritance is nice but it need not be a basket of dogmas and retrograde thinking. We need to remove many of our religious and cultural beliefs that have become outdated. Can we still condone child marriages and honor killing under the sanction of the religion? Can we want our visits to restaurants and clubs be vitiated by some orthodox tenet of segregating men and women? Can we order the many food companies to employ people of a particular caste or religion because of 'untouchables' considerations? We need to become more scientific than cultural, more democratic than religious.
7. **It is not cricket "Only":** There are other things to life too. We must get off the frivolous and get onto substantial. There are nice things like cricket, Bollywood and religious festivals but more important are things like education, industrial development and quality of life that we must actively look for and demand.
8. **Centralized control:** Our "Socialistic pattern" of society was built around unity of command and control in everything. We voted in the name of charismatic leaders for fifty years, letting that leader (rather than a council of leaders) wielding all the power. Our political policy and processes followed this pattern. So everything got decided at the top of hierarchy. No devolution of power from center to state, or from state governments to city councils or panchayats. For such a large country, the futility of such an approach should have been self-evident. This 'span of control' did not work for communism; it hasn't work for us either. Need for a *decentralized, efficient and inclusive system.*
9. **Reservations:** It was never solely a matter of distribution of fruits of national progress. It was more about scaling than distribution. You cannot uplift hundreds of millions out of poverty by reserving a few thousand jobs. But if hundred millions of more jobs are created, you can direct many millions at the deserving poor. Reservations were not the panacea for the under- achievement of a

particular social group, creating more opportunities was. For shortage of engineering seats in colleges, we needed to establish more engineering colleges, not keep redistributing seats. Rather than using reservations to provide a short-term amelioration of unequal opportunity, these have been misused to award political patronage to vote banks. Now long-term reservations have become addictive and are considered as an entitlement. To bring in meritocracy, incentive based schemas are needed to be introduced to unleash our million bright minds from all sections of the society onto the world stage.

10. **Problems solving:** (rather than building the future) Our efforts cannot remain focused on solving problems, removing earlier disparities, cleaning older cities, improving our education, rather than building new technologies, processes and systems, new areas of endeavor. We need to focus more (80 per cent as per Pareto basics) in creating the new avenues of future.

11. **Solving the wrong problems:** Even worse than "Problem Solving", our leadership has become adept at solving non-issues, as long as that perpetuates their gains (electoral and sometimes financial). Predilection towards solvable problems rather than critical problems, i.e. low hanging fruit is the norm. For the gullible majority, politicians say and do what the public wants to hear and see rather than what the public need. The government would prefer to control institutions of higher learning (AIIMS, IIMs, IITs) while the critical problem is in the primary education system. The problem is deficient capacity in high school education, but we label it as inequality between various sections of society and institute misguided reservations. The problem is lack of focus in job creation and we spent all our time crafting poverty alleviation schemes in kind, where 90 per cent benefits leak out. The problem is regulations prohibiting free movement of commodities, and we fashion a public distribution channel (ration

shops), which perhaps is the most wasteful system in the world. The examples are many where substantial resources are applied to wrong problems. It is like doing *by-pass surgery to a patient with a lung problem. Now both lung and heart have ailments*. A crying need is to bring government's *attention to real issues* rather than irrelevant problem solving.

12. **Our fascination with Heroes and 'Don't Care' for the ordinary:** The 'Hero worship' by general public has reached crazy proportions due to the multi-channel TV and social media on the internet. We seem to have picked up wrong role models. We don't hear the worthies like Narayana Murthy or Ratan Tata as much as we hear some film and sports stars (with due regards to their exceptional performance in their fields). Our politicians serve up a continuous barrage of their being patriotic and servants of the people. But in effect, the progress agenda of the general public has never been taken up. Till we believe each word that they say, and don't think for ourselves, we will land up following their self centered agenda and not the agenda for India's progress.

So if we apply our thoughts, effort and time to creating positive patterns by remaining focused on real issues, and obliterating negative patterns by eliminating/reducing attention/effort on non-issues, we will be able to augment the positive factors in all strategy areas and ameliorate the negative factors.

Who do we think will do this? Will our government suddenly become savvy and people oriented (as millions are expecting to happen)? Will the people of India take the matter into their hands and start taking mature collective decisions (rather than being swayed by retrograde non-issues)? That is what the future will show us and that is what will determine whether India comes out triumphant (closer to Value 1) or diminished (closer to Value 7).

# 8

# Unraveling the Riddle: Who will it be, to Make Dream 2050 Possible

> **Montage:** is a technique in film editing which a series of short shots are edited into a sequence to condense space, time, and information. It is usually used to suggest the passage of time. (Wikipedia, The free Encyclopedia)

### The Different Perspectives of the Leaders and the Led

> Montage, in film making, is the art of cutting one image to next and next, and so on. This is the real art in the hands of a film director. Whereas audience is focused on the content of a frame, it is in director's hand to twist and change context and take the narrative in another direction. (Alfred Hitchcock)

In politics, exactly the same art is practiced with gusto for another purpose. The montage is in the hands of political power centers. When the general public is trying to understand their present agendas (contents of the frame), the next pronouncement morphs the narrative to something different (suitable to the interests of the power centers).

The montage that the public (or any other ensemble, e.g., workers, middle class, technologists, citizens of Maharashtra, and so on) have in mind is better quality of life (including education for kids, professional growth, and peaceful environment). The political forces can read the contents of this frame. If it is not too disruptive for their narrative, they might even incorporate it in their own story. If not, a way must be found to ignore public narrative and continue playing the political narrative.

The public has Hobson's choice. They can either accept the current political narrative or wait till the next elections to show their rejection of the narrative; unless the political power has (temporarily) introduced Mcguffins and/or modified the montage a little bit to look like the one public has on their mind. There will always be time to twist the montage to the normal political color again, soon.

### Who Finally Wins

So which of the two montages wins? Are politicians able to twist and turn it to keep the majority occupied in colorful contents and get their own montage going? Are the people able to coerce the governing entities to adopt their montage?

Do the 'push and pull' keep bringing cyclical ups and downs? Does a synergic and mutually adjusting upward curve define the composite montage? Or is it antagonist and discordant downward curve? Which one predominates, political power or people power? What happens in long term? Say in 2050.

Let us focus on two extreme scenarios (like we did for projections). The best situation is when all is good, i.e. the two montages are being respected, understood and adjusted for synergic best outcomes.

The other one is exactly opposite. The montages are antagonistic, trying to force the other montage to back down and force their own patterns on the other. The result is a conflict situation.

**Scenario 1:** If the two montage sequences try to tune in and synchronize, there is a possibility of constant modification of the two montage versions so that they asymptotically merge in the long term (say on 2050). The synergic modification and improvement in the two will result in the positive growth curve for both and the environment too.

**Scenario 2:** If they do not (it can take place if the political power centers refuse to honor the public sentiments or vice versa), the confrontation becomes the norm. The polity may have an upper hand in the short term, but sooner or later will have to bite the dust. Unless the whole polity is beyond repair, the hit and trial begins till the conforming political structure emerges. But meanwhile, the nation's efforts have been used up towards solving political problems and not employed in the progress of the nation. How much time this 'hit and trial' takes is anyone's guess. It may be just one election or centuries of fratricidal civil wars or many possibilities in between.

Who wields the real power in this battle of influence?

Let us enunciate our inference first. In a democratic setup, It is necessarily the voter or people or majority. If "Sarv Jan Hitay, Sarv Jan Sukhay" (universal benefit and happiness for all citizens) does not actually happen, the government in power will be short lived and a new selection process will begin.

If the selection process itself is compromised and keeps throwing wrong political dispensations, the public may rise against the process itself.

One way or the other, the voters (majority) wins in a democracy, in the long run.

### Why are We Enamored with the Concept of Montage

It is not just another fashionable (and exotic) concept that has prompted the usage of montage simile here. It encapsulates good v/s bad, long-term v/s short-term trade offs so well, that we feel compelled to bring it in for our discussions. We routinely see the parents struggling (and sometimes arguing with their kids' school teachers) for higher marks in the half yearly maths examinations, middle class clamoring for lower tax for a particular commercial transaction in a particular year and rural bourgeois believing the politicians promises for reservations and loan waivers. Too occupied with these short-term contents on single frame of information, we for that moment forget that this frame is just one of the many in the long sequence of lifelong montage.

Each event is just a small particle in the whole story. In terms of montage, what is important is how your child turns out in life (with or without high marks in mid term maths exam), or whether the taxation regime is slowly tuning in with the citizens' per capita income (and inflation) or remains predatory; or whether the banking system can take the impact of populist loan wavers or sink the whole economy and effectively make us all paupers.

So if we look at the events, keeping in view that these are just frames on a montage, we can look at events more objectively while keeping the macro perspective cogent and firmly in sight.

### Where can the Current Political Montage Take us in 2050

The current state of political activity and discourse is more tilted towards Dismal Scenario 2050. We have lack of a progressive agenda (economic development, diplomatic dexterity, military effectiveness and infrastructure scaling) and a plethora of regressive activity (divisive, caste ridden politics, corruption, inefficiency, policy paralysis). This will have to change to a new plot with a whole lot of environment building that includes policies and governance, infrastructure, enablers, education and training, continuity assurance, etc.

### Who will do it

It is a lot of hard work for a long time.

The major contributors in this great expedition could be all or some of the following categories of people.

1. Polity and Bureaucracy.
2. Intelligentsia; scientists, educationists, philosophers, opinion makers, statesmen, social scientists.
3. Industrialists, film stars, rich players, others with large endowments.
4. Current generation industry workers and other salaried middle class.
5. Next generation workers and middle class (People born 2000 onwards).
6. Future generations (People born in 2020s and beyond).

These stake players have differing leverages, different interests and different stakes at various times in future. Let us take a look at a representative picture of how these categories look at various aspects of the India story (the figure below gives a 'sense of the issue' and is not a methodical measure for the parameters or their values mentioned).

We have used a scale of 1 to 5 for parameter values. The assigned values are estimates in line with current state of affairs. It can be argued that the parameter value estimation deserves finer granularity. But keeping matters simple, we try to get the 'sense of the issue' rather than analytic details.

### Who Holds the Key Today

Drawing upon the conclusions reached in our earlier analysis, the following table encapsulates the current scenario, except that we try to give a 'sense' of the influence that forthcoming and future generations will exert on the various issues.

The salient observations are

1. The financial and administrative leverage is vested with the polity, bureaucracy and industrial scions. The bourgeois has hardly any leverage in decision taking processes.
2. Consequently, the opportunity and capacity for bringing about change is all vested in the polity, governance system and big business.

One may argue that we are not giving due credence to the thriving democracy in India, that so many sing paeans about on daily basis. But we are not disregarding the power of democratic forces. The fact remains that the exercise of democratic power by the vast majority is post the event (i.e. after the government has consistently failed for five years, the majority can vote them out).

Even then, the Indian democracy is more about form than essence. The amount of drum beating that we have about free and fair elections, cannot hide the fact that the elected representative are not the best leaders that India can throw up. In fact, there is no systematic pyramid building in the electoral process. Even the politicians do not know who the next chief minister or the prime minister is till the horse-trading is over and done with. Many shortcomings ail the whole electoral and selection process, but more details will take us away from the point that we want to make. And the point is that the financial/ administrative leverage remains vested with polity, governance

## Who will be the Harbingers of Change in India Story

| S. No. ↓ | Class of Society → <br> Parameter ↓ | Polity and Bureaucracy | Industrialists and others with Large Endowments | Intelligentsia | Current Generation Workers + Salaried Middle Class | Next generation Workers + Middle class (born 2000 owards) | Future Generations (born 2020 onwards) |
|---|---|---|---|---|---|---|---|
| | **Who holds the strings now** | | | | | | |
| P1 | Current financial leverage | 5 | 5 | 3 | 3 | 2 | 1 |
| P2 | Current leverage over "common Assets" including public assets | 4 | 4 | 1 | 1 | 1 | 1 |
| P3 | Present capacity for including change | 3 | 4 | 4 | 2 | 1 | 1 |
| P4 | Opportunity for inducing change | 4 | 4 | 5 | 2 | 4 | 5 |
| | **Total Positive Leverage** | **16** | **17** | **13** | **8** | **8** | **8** |

structure and big business. And their interests may not be congruent with the vast majority, especially with the coming generations, who do not have any leverage (or supporters) at all at this moment in history.

## Who can Hamper the March of India

Looking at a similar table (it gives a clear idea in one look), let us see who has a larger interest in status quo.

### Who will be the Harbingers of Change in India Story

| S. No. → | Class of Society → Parameter → | Polity and Bureaucracy | Industrialists and others with large endowments | Intelligentsia | Current Generation workers + salaried middle class | Next generation workers + middle class (born 2000 owards) | Future generations (born 2020 onwards) |
|---|---|---|---|---|---|---|---|
| | **Who can put a spoke in the wheel** | | | | | | |
| N1 | Current comfort level with status quo | 5 | 3 | 2 | 1 | 1 | 1 |
| N2 | Leverage for maintaining status quo | 3 | 3 | 2 | 2 | 1 | 1 |
| N3 | Capacity for creating road blocks for change | 3 | 3 | 2 | 1 | 1 | 1 |
| N4 | Motivation for blocking change | 5 | 4 | 2 | 1 | 1 | 1 |
| | **Total Negative Leverage** | **16** | **13** | **8** | **5** | **4** | **4** |

No surprises here. Whosoever has the disproportionate leverage, will like to retain it unless one is threatened by retribution (democratically). So the polity, bureaucracy and entrenched big business will like to stop any movement where their control over matters is threatened.

## Who is the Most Impacted: Who will Spur India's Growth

No surprises here either. The entrenched interests, which wish to perpetuate their interests without ensuring widespread

### Who will be the Harbingers of Change in India Story

| S. No. → | Class of Society → Parameter → | Polity and Bureaucracy | Industrialists and others with Large Endowments | Intelligentsia | Current Generation Workers + Salaried Middle Class | Next Generation Workers + Middle Class (born 2000 owards) | Future Generations (born 2020 onwards) |
|---|---|---|---|---|---|---|---|
| | **Whose life is it? Who will galvanize India story?** | | | | | | |
| M1 | Possibility of improvement in life | 1 | 2 | 2 | 5 | 5 | 5 |
| M2 | Motivation for change | 1 | 2 | 4 | 5 | 5 | 5 |
| M3 | Intellectual capacity | 3 | 4 | 5 | 3 | 4 | 5 |
| M4 | Capability for enabling India for global competition | 2 | 3 | 3 | 4 | 5 | 5 |
| | **Total Negative Leverage** | **7** | **11** | **14** | **17** | **19** | **20** |

prosperity and progress, are not the best qualified or motivated to take India into the high league.

The current political and administrative dispensations may not fit the bill for leading India to top slot by 2050 (especially as they are lacking on both capability and inclination). It is more likely that the general public will be forced to bring in political dispensations that will. And most of the democratic exercise of power will be accomplished not by the current fragmented vote banks, but the younger generations who are coalesced by the dream of a 'Great India' rather than divided by inconsequential issues.

## Prognosis Going Forward

The responsibility for building a new India will be predominantly borne by the younger generations for two reasons.

Firstly, the older generations have lesser capability (education wise) for understanding, accepting and internalizing the ever quickening change. In addition, unlearning the embedded conventional malpractices and then changing over to new processes and paradigms is easier said than done.

Secondly, the younger generations have a bigger stake in India doing well. After all, they will be in the middle of the challenge (and wage earners) in another 20/30 years. Elders, if they still are living (with all their baggage of old fashioned ideas), are more likely to be supine dependents on the younger generation for their living.

So it is a clear cut line of responsibility. The general public and predominantly the younger generation, who will have more say in the political and economic environment buildup that will take India to new heights of glory.

The younger generation will also make the hands-on contribution by becoming the millions of economy workers, educationists, military personnel, administrators and even new generation of political leaders.

We are talking about a long-term perspective of fifty years from today to mid of this century. So the young people, who are in their 20s and 30s today, will be the harbingers of change right now. In twenty years, they would have graduated to positions of senior administrators, managers, policy experts, philosophers and guides. Meanwhile, they would have educated, guided and directed the next generation of young people and passed on the mantle. The process will repeat ad-infinitum. The hope is that there would be smooth handover from one generation to another. But "tragedy of commons" is always threatening to undo this 'laminar' flow and induce eddies of grabbing and looting in between, causing social disturbances on the way.

As Jack Welch says on clear thinking, "We must face reality as it is and not as we wish it to be". Well, the reality is that the present day state of affairs in India leaves much to be desired in respect of our ability to be world beaters by 2050. And we need to do something substantial soon.

We have a stern warning in the words of Albert Einstein, "If you keep doing what you are doing, you will keep getting the results you are getting". Articulating in today's colloquial terms, "If nothing changes, nothing changes". So if we have the great expectations of our future, that future beckons us to become great as well. (Never seen a great country with a third grade thought processes or people or education or technology and so on.) So better get on with it. Go change India and environment to get there in 2050.

### What should We Become, to Do It

So what would we look like, (if) when we have taken India to greatness by 2050? (Old timers please excuse; if I seem to identifying more with the young Indians in this discussion). So what will be our profile, as individuals, as governance body, as a society and as a nation? (It may look like an enunciation of imperatives for the younger generation in these roles.)

### Profile as Young Individuals

1. Hard-working erudite women/men, engaged in maximizing their capabilities and skills. (India should have at least 800 million of them in 2050.)
2. Engaged in furthering their careers and pursuit of happiness by fair means in industry and service. Not

blindly pursuing money and instant gratification at the cost of moral turpitude.

3. Ready to stand up for democratic rights and against social ills. Will contribute voluntarily to activities for common good.
4. Conscientious voter. Consider voting as a solemn duty to bring in a fair and progressive government. Will not be swayed by caste, class and color considerations or by other kinds of inducements. Will actively oppose and speak against Mcguffins in use by various political/social outfits.
5. Put the nation above the society, society before the family and family before self. Will appreciate patriotic duty, obligations to the society and commitment to the family.
6. Committed to excelling in all walks of life, becoming nonpareil scientists, teachers, philosophers, thought leaders, artists, managers, entertainers, researchers. and so on.

### Profile as Young Politicians

7. Sworn to duties and responsibilities for the nation and society (actually understanding and internalizing the 'Oath of office'). Seekers of self actualization as statesmen and servants of the people and nation. (India needs a many thousands of them.)
8. Knowledgeable, erudite, committed men/women with strategic thought and unwavering commitment to the common good. Always learning, interfacing, monitoring and pushing for whatever is good for the nation and the society.
9. Uncompromising zeal for pushing for progress and subduing the retrograde schools of thought. Capacity for retaining positive thought even during the most serious adversity. No personal agendas, when considering national matters.

10. Capability and willingness to lead and motivate the populace for progressive initiatives, despite their ignorance, unwillingness and hesitation. Commitment to follow up on strategic plans and programs, with disregard for personal gains, popularity or earning favors with political dispensations.
11. Capability and training/education to interface with a wide spectrum of accomplished people; in industry, bureaucracy, foreign diplomats, opinion makers, academia, social workers, other global leaders, philanthropists, and many more. To be open to diverse ideas and opinions and be able to induce a consensual inference amongst conflicting interests.
12. Intellectual prowess for seeing what the others might not. Ability to sense opportunities and challenges and thinking of novel ideas, solutions and methodologies for seizing opportunities and tackling challenges.

### Profile as Young Bureaucrats

13. True to role and assignment received. Able to learn and adapt to assigned role, location, audience and the macro level national policy picture together. Ability for a life on a steep learning curve for a higher value and challenging assignments in emerging functional areas. (Needed a few million of highest level intellect)
14. Service orientation towards public. Should measure own success by how many have benefited from the facilitation provided. Should become a part of the 'Brand Equity' of the governance setup. Should be able to pursue this under any political dispensation.
15. Academically accomplished, logical, process oriented, motivated women/men, committed to placing India in the highest league.
16. Beyond the lure of political patronage, easy gains, fearless enough to face the inimical intent of the illicit attitudes, able to focus on the public good even while being bombarded by distractions, insinuations, ire of entrenched interests and competitors.

17. Intellectually inspired to look for new opportunities, endeavors, and instruments of innovation for the ability to put and keep India at the head of the committee of nations.
18. Actively engaged with global polity and decision makers in understanding the global scenario and finding the best place for India to assume her role and position.

**Profile as Young Entrepreneurs**

19. Hard-working erudite women/men, engaged in maximizing the industrial power and technological supremacy of India by employing their capabilities and skills. (India should have at least a few million of them in 2050.)
20. Academic excellence for high tech and intellectual pursuits. Have an open mind to continuously upgrade knowledge and skills. Are ready to learn new technologies. Ready to spawn new ideas, business processes and initiatives for high tech services and systems.
21. Passion and perseverance for being the global 'best of breed', in technology, methods and processes and efficiency. Willing to co-operate, collaborate and assist for industry's common good.
22. Blessed with a spirit of adventure rather than being a 9 to 5 camp-follower. Ability to take risks.
23. Focused on excellence and quality rather than profitability. Has a commitment for sustainability, environment and social responsibility.

**Profile as Young Professionals**

24. Qualified and hard-working engineers/doctors/ researchers pursuing the development and deployment of technology, systems, products and services in all areas of endeavor. (India should have many millions of them in 2050.)
25. Passion and perseverance for researching new knowledge and concepts, technology and process architectures.

26. Networked with peers and competitors for pushing the envelope of the 'state of the art' globally. Ability to think of the new capabilities, rather than getting limited by current requirements.
27. Focused on futuristic advancement more than commercial aspects.
28. Focused on continuous improvement.

**Profile as Young Citizens**

29. Conscientious family person, building a happy home for themselves, children and other family members. Able to cast away stereotypes of man/woman division of work and be an equal hands-on parent. Be willing contributors to quality of life and environment protection for the sake of future generations. Also sustainable lifestyle for the family by building assets and savings for meeting health, sustenance and life enrichment requirements. (We should have 1.5 billion such citizens.)
30. Be an active member of the larger family, i.e. the society. Active for social causes and welfare activities. Be an ardent helper in creating a secure and prosperous future for own children and others in the next generation by ensuring participation in creation of utilities, cultural events and local administration.
31. Proud of our heritage, about the enormous wisdom enshrined in old scripture, religious tolerance, Vedic way of frugal but happy living, and boundless imagination like the builders of Taj or historic forts. At the same time, takes a stand against the bag of cults, religious mumbo jumbo and falsified historical narrative as being paddled by the inept but devious public figures.
32. Believer in the Gandhian adage "Do unto your neighbor, what you expect your neighbor to do unto you". Practice of reciprocal behavior, even at the cost of inconvenience. Willing to play by the rules of the law and conforming to social etiquettes. Helping the

government agencies with their functions by assisting whenever required.

*Well, then, we know what we need to do in various roles that we can assume in the society and as professionals in the coming years. Hope we Indians will rise to the occasion.*

So young India, It is up to you, to know, to think and to act.

And Get India to a Happy 2050.

# Epilogue

As we live through the coming years and decades, we will get to know how the thoughts and projections of various thinkers, leaders, economists and experts pan out. We will also know about the "Black Swans" that could hinder India's roll towards prosperity or sudden 'updrafts' of air that could provide a lucky sudden rise in India's fortune.

There will accordingly be heroes and villains along the line, but the story is likely to reach the happy ending with the concerted efforts of 1.5 billion Indians, as more than one billion of them will be in their productive phases of life during this journey. But that can happen if and only if the first steps are taken now. We must start reinforcing the positive factors and mitigating the negative ones right now. There is no time to wait, because our demographic advantage may fritter away meanwhile, if we hedge our bets for too long.

It should be our intention to stay engaged with the process of India's rise for the next few decades and spread the message. Maybe it will pay to make a larger section of the populace in India aware about the actual achievements v/s milestones, so that any laggards could pull up and momentum could be maintained.

As India goes forward, there will be shedding the old and emergence of the new. Dislodging entrenched interests, divisive civics, corruption, shortages, inefficiencies, we should banish just every kind of mediocrity. Injecting new ideas, the new generations of Indian experts/workers/intellectuals, new technologies, new processes, new statecraft, we should boost all dimensions of our capabilities.

Hope this discussion will induce many to jump into thinking and acting for creating a Dream India 2050 and beyond.

Let us finish with some words from Jawaharlal Nehru for inspiration:

> The past brings us many gifts; indeed, all we have today of culture, civilization, science or knowledge of some aspect of truth, is a gift of distant or recent past to us. It is right that we acknowledge our obligation to the past. But the past does not exhaust our duty or obligation. We owe a duty to future also, and perhaps that obligation is greater than the one we owe to the past. For the past is past and done with, we cannot change it; the future is yet to come and perhaps we will be able to shape it a little. If the past have given us a part of the truth, the future also hides many aspects of the truth, and invites us to search for them. But often the past is jealous of the future and holds us in a terrible grip, and we have to struggle with it to get free to face and advance towards the future.

# Appendices

## APPENDIX "A"
## PROGRESS DASHBOARD INFORMATION MODEL: MACRO LEVEL VIEW (STRATEGY AREAS AND FACTORS)

The description in this appendix provides the structure of information model and also the methodology of construction of the Progress Dashboard display to present the macro level indicators on that display.

We have mentioned the structure of information model in the beginning of Chapter 4 (Page 53). Let us now map the structure onto our Dashboard Display.

Status of India's progress

⇩

Five strategy areas

⇩

Five positive and five negative factors for each of the strategy areas

⇩

Five sub-factors of each of the positive and negative factors

Status of India's progress is our "Progress Dashboard" itself. The five strategy areas are the five boxes on the display, two in the upper half and three in the bottom half. The five positive factors are displayed as bars in the left half of each box and five negative factors on the right. We defer the discussion on sub-factors to Appendix "B".

To begin constructing the Dashboard, let us now enumerate the five strategy areas and five positive and five negative factors for each strategy areas, to be placed on the Dashboard.

The five strategy areas (as defined in Chapter 4, Page 55) are:

A. Political and Regulatory Environment

B. Economy and Business

C. People and Capability Development

D. Strategic Assets: Natural and Man-made Resources

E. External and Internal Security.

Let us now elaborate each of the strategy areas by enumerating factors.

## A. Factors: Political and Regulatory Environment

The most important of the strategy areas that outlines what and how a nation plans to do for growth and prosperity. This dimension has an effect on all other strategy areas, which are shown on the Dashboard.

The factors that make up this strategy area are:

### *Positive Factors*

1. India's Brand Equity
2. Enabling Policy Framework
3. Governance Structure
4. Quality of Environment
5. Synergistic Relationships.

### *Negative Factors*

1. Bad Politics
2. Reactive in Responding to Challenges
3. Lack of Planning and Program Implementation
4. Corruption
5. Tragedy of the Commons.

Let us draw a pictorial representation of the strategic area "Political and Regulatory Environment", showing the five positive factors on the left side and the five negative factors on the right side. The bars below each of these factors provide us the computed (from weighted sum of its sub-factors) value of each of these factors to be represented as a 'fuzzy scale' value from indices one to five. To recap, these may or may not be linear values, e.g. 1/2/3/4/5 or some percentages, but can be piecewise consistent values, e.g. no/may-be-not/probably/may-be/yes or any other fuzzy theoretic value. The top of the color bar is the value. The lower portion of the bar is filled with the same color for nice presentation.

But hereon, for ease of understanding, we map these fuzzy values to a linear scale of 1 to 5 (we use fuzzy concept for cogent representation on the Dashboard but will avoid fuzzy mathematics computation complexity, remembering yet again to 'keep things simple').

Each factor (positive or negative) has an assigned weight (at the moment, the weights have been assigned in tune with the preceding discussions, but can be varied while discussing dissimilar scenarios, now or later). The factor value multiplied by weight gives us the factor effect. All positive factor effects when aggregated, give us the positive weight of that strategic area, and negative weight is obtained likewise. The positive minus the negative weights give us the generic state of affairs in that strategic area. This is shown in the last row as Total Factor Contribution (abbreviated TFC).

It goes without saying that for becoming a world leader, you should carry more positive weight (literally) in every strategy area. At least, one should be 'best in class' or thereabout for being up there.

So this is the stencil we use for filling up values later, after some analysis of the Indian scenario.

[The value shown now are only for explaining the stencil, we will come to real values later.]

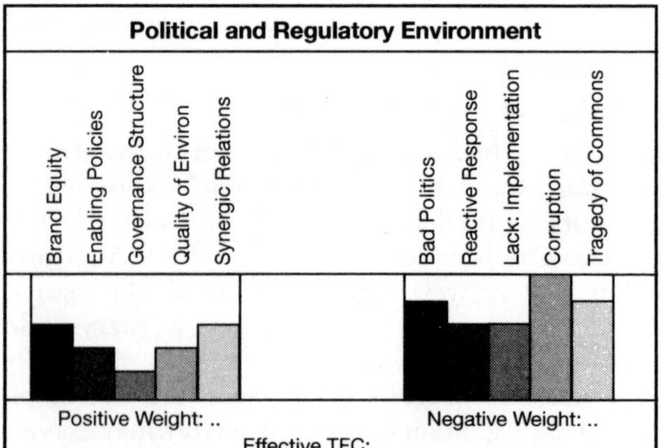

## B. Factors: Economy and Business

Now we come to the specific domain areas that create the nation's prosperity. Economy, income, productivity and quality of life are cardinal to greatness of a nation. The factors that make up this strategy areas are:

### *Positive Factors*

1. Economy Size and Growth
2. Immunity from Global Downturn
3. Private Sector Excellence
4. Development of Industrial Clusters
5. Diversified Economy.

### *Negative Factors*

1. Red Tape
2. Technology Dependency
3. Lack of Excellence
4. Low Buyer Sophistication
5. Denial Regime.

Similar pictorial representation of this central strategic area is as given below:

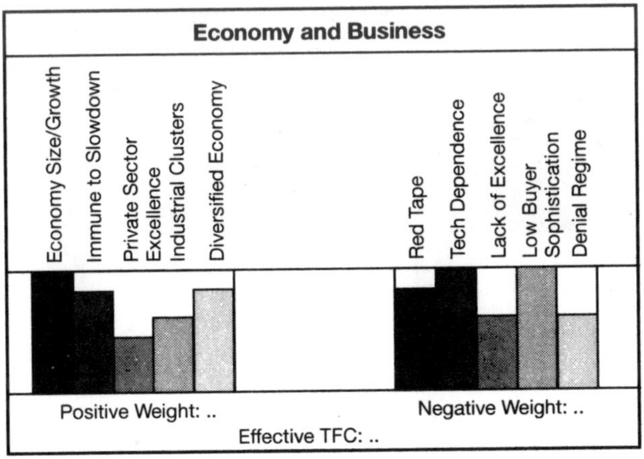

## C. Factors: People and Capability Development

The human assets are the instruments of execution in all strategy areas, so are the basic pre-requisite for excellence in all strategy areas. The various factors affecting this strategy area are mentioned below.

### *Positive Factors*

1. Demographic Advantage
2. English Speaking Majority
3. Education and Training
4. Preference for Engineering
5. Lifestyle Enrichment.

### *Negative Factors*

1. Poor Primary Education
2. Poor Budgetary Support for Education
3. No R&D Excellence
4. Reservations without Aim
5. Lack of Systems Thinking: "Jugaad".

Pictorial representation of this people centric strategic area is as given below.

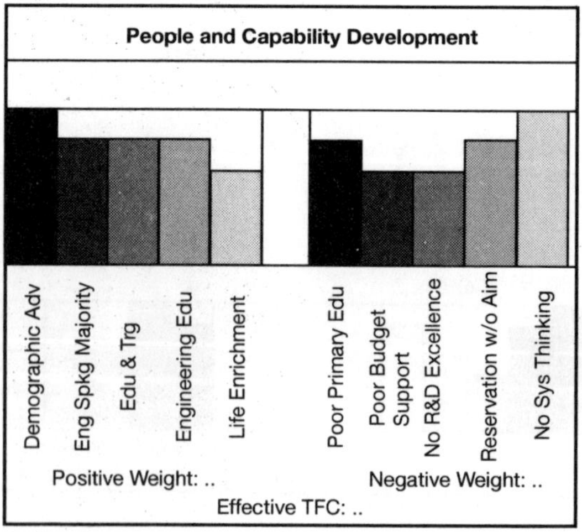

### D. Factors: Strategic Assets: Natural and Man-made Resources

The natural and man-made assets are the foundations on which the human resources can deploy their aggregate skills.

The important factors in this strategy area are as follows:

***Positive Factors***

1. Abundant Natural Resources
2. Enablers for Industry
3. Financial System
4. Educational and Research
5. Life Experience Improvement.

***Negative Factors***

1. Unclear Division of Responsibilities
2. Rehabilitation
3. Bad Urban Infrastructure
4. Low Investment in Infrastructure
5. Process Paralysis.

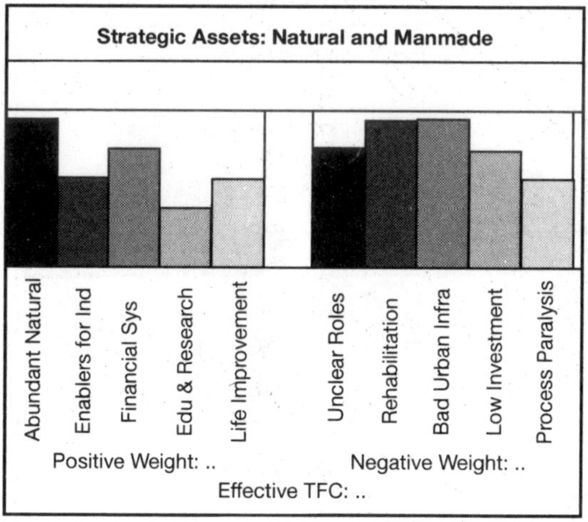

## E. Factors: External and Internal Security

The other strategy areas can prosper if they can continue performing their progress inducing activities without interruption or disruptions from inimical factors. The factors for enabling such a continuity assurance are as follows:

### *Positive Factors*

1. An Established Military Force
2. Security Infrastructure
3. Structure, Processes and Systems
4. Operational Robustness
5. Evolution of Technology.

### *Negative Factors*

1. Old Mindsets
2. Value Approach Missing
3. Asset Aggregation Mindset
4. Pro-Active Reorientation Lacking
5. Missing Synergic Coordination.

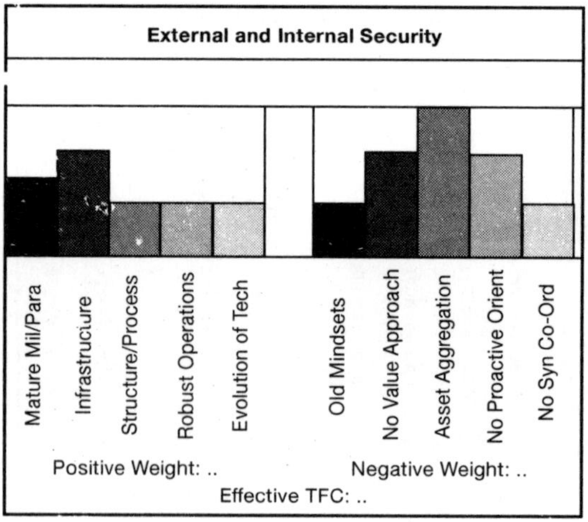

Putting all the strategy areas display together, now we have the "Progress Dashboard" display.

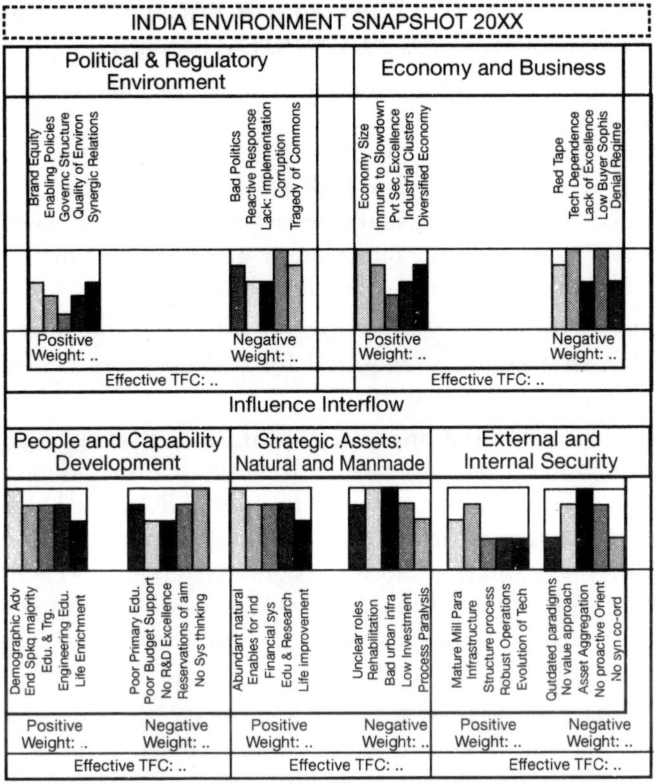


The influence interflow window indicates the possibility that the strategy areas can influence each others. There could be dependencies at factor level or even at sub-factor levels that can be represented with connectors to this Influence Interflow window. For the time being however, we choose to keep this discussion limited to only knowing the possibility of interflow for the sake of simplicity.

## APPENDIX "B"

## PROGRESS DASHBOARD INFORMATION MODEL: DRILLING DOWN TO LEVEL 3 (SUB-FACTORS), WEIGHT ASSIGNMENT AND COMPUTATION METHOD

To understand the underlying logic of our Dashboard information model, we have already enumerated the five 'Strategic areas', and five positive and five negative factors that combine to make up the overall effect in a strategy area in Appendix "A". To increase the accuracy and granularity in our 'Efficacy Estimation' in each strategy area, we now drill down to the third level of detail, namely sub-factors.

This methodology can be extended to even fourth or fifth level, but that could be required for a deeper analysis rather than a concept work like this.

We enumerate the important sub-factors that aggregate to form a factor. This will ensure that we are including most micro level issues in our factor definition and estimation. Each of these sub-factors may have different importance for the factor that it is a part of, so we assign a weightage to each sub-factor in the enumeration list in brackets. We discuss the computations of various values at the end of this appendix.

While enumerating sub-factors, we will have to become more India specific too. We have a chosen 250 most pertinent sub-factors, out of a possibility of many thousand micro level issues. Hopefully, the chosen sub-factors reflect the current India scenario accurately. As we traverse the progress curve, some sub-factors (which are not in the list now) can pop-up in importance, while some on the list can drop off the list because they are not in the top five category.

Also to reiterate, the per cent contribution is our estimate at this time, all these parameters will need to be updated as India moves up on the progress curve.

### A. Factors → Sub-Factors: Political and Regulatory Environment

#### *Positive Factors*

1. **India's Brand Equity**
   a. Stable democracy. (30%)

   b. Intellectual prowess of political leadership. (15%)
   c. Proven excellence in IT and knowledge services. (20%)
   d. Quality of engineering talent. (25%)
   e. Cultural richness and advance civilization of the past. (10%)

2. **Enabling Policy Framework**
   a. Clear enunciation of long-term business policy. (20%)
   b. Transparent and easy interface with regulatory system. (40%)
   c. Two-way interaction with business and trade promotion entities. (10%)
   d. Effective recourse for grievance amelioration, legal/administrative. (20%)
   e. Instruments for participation in evolving policy upgrade. (10%)

3. **Governance Structure**
   a. Transparent governance structure with well-publicized areas of assistive influence and responsibilities. (25%)
   b. Easy access at all levels, from working to policy level. (35%)
   c. Automation of procedures including web enabled services. (15%)
   d. Predictable iteration cycle time and assured service levels. (15%)
   e. Coordination with related governance entities and trade organizations. (10%)

4. **Quality of Environment**
   a. Erudite, resolute, forward looking, industry friendly intelligentsia, politicians, think tanks, mentors, researchers, academia trade organizations. (35%)
   b. Social harmony, cultural cohesiveness, religious freedom, social organizations, non-profits. (15%)

c. Educational opportunities, citizens' zeal to excel and further national interests. (20%)

d. Opportunities for earning and excelling by merit; ease of overcoming social inequities. (20%)

e. Law and order, security of assets, freedom of ownership and action. (10%)

5. **Synergistic Relationships**

a. Political pacts and strategic alliances with other nations. (30%)

b. Economic pacts with other nations and trade groups. (30%)

c. Intra-nation federal (center-state) relationship. (10%)

d. Strategic relationships with big businesses. (15%)

e. Industry relations with innovators, academia research. (15%)

### *Negative Factors*

1. **Bad Politics**

a. Absence of statesmen, nationalistic leadership. (20%)

b. Invasion of politics by opportunists, interested in perpetuating their own hold over power rather than progress of the nation. (25%)

c. Divisive (caste, reservations, etc.) and exploitative (in the garb of welfare schemes, but used for diverting resources) manifestos of political parties with no place for issues that matter, e.g. economics. education, R&D, job creation, defense, infrastructure, etc. (20%)

d. Cantankerous, obstructive conduct of lawmakers during policy and law enactment. Delays in or absence of pro-active policy formulation. (20%)

e. No industry/domain/issue champions in the political class. (15%)

2. **Reactive in Responding to Challenges**
    a. Discretionary policies, hence no process based automated decision making for programmable events. (20%)
    b. Centralized decision making. So every major or minor decision must traverse the whole chain of command. Hence, tardy and often 'beyond use time frame' decisions. (25%)
    c. Response to 'Black Swan' events perhaps 'worst in class'. Generally, 'off the cuff' decision by person on site. Most of the times the decision is to wait and watch, e.g. hijacking to Kandhahar, terrorist attacks, events at Davos, joining Asean all smack of inaction rather than proactive action. (25%)
    d. Response slaved to vote bank politics rather than securing the future, e.g. FDI, Nano factory at Singur, nuclear treaty, inaction against Chinese incursions, avoiding counteraction against extremists for the fear of religious backlash are the burning examples. (15%)
    e. Persistence of pre-independence practices and mental blocks despite overhaul of regulatory environment, e.g. spittoons in software centers, hardcopy of emails in file, we cannot give up our old fixations and dogmas. (10%)
3. **Lack of Planning and Program Implementation**
    a. No top down structured plan for most of governance. No declared roadmaps. No open scrutiny or consultation in planning process, e.g. big plans are hand down from an inscrutable government to a 'tail clear' keeping own turf safe bureaucracy, so except aggressive proclamation there is hardly any movement on ground. (30%)
    b. Emphasis on problem solving and not on future progress, e.g. one is more likely to hear poverty alleviation and job guarantee program rather than job creation in emerging sectors or research. (15%)

c. Delay in implementation, e.g. each functionary not a part of a system team, but a power center. There is no thread of continuity between the intents of top level, middle rung leaders and operational people. The results compliance is not a major requirement. Spending budgets by itself is compliance, the efficacy or actual value delivered not scrutinized. (20%)

d. Bottoms up implementation (at the discretion of lowest level functionaries) is rampant and the result is low quality (but quantitatively billable) with huge rework requirement, e.g. digging up the same area for many services is a norm. (20%)

e. Leakage and corruption spawning the downstream corruption, inefficiency and malpractices, and shutting out the innovative, e.g. SME sector shut out from providing specially tailored and effectively localized solutions to the social sector. (15%)

**4. Corruption**

a. Moral corruption. Self before everyone or everything else. Self perpetuation becomes the basic aim. Neither progress nor the common good remain anywhere on the radar. (20%)

b. Monetary corruption. Diversion of public funds meant for some other purpose. Extracting money for providing public services, taking bribes for twisting rules to benefit the undeserving or letting someone disproportionate advantage. (20%)

c. Misuse of position. Allowing someone undeserving access to positions of power, positions of benefit or shielding someone from the rule of law when she/he has committed some crime. (20%)

d. Inaction or delay to benefit someone. Not acting and letting someone evade responsibility or punishment. Delaying things in a way to harm the interest of deserving and benefit the undeserving. (20%)

e. Acts of omission. Having the responsibility and capability to further the interests of the nation or society but willfully omitting to do it. Unfortunately, not doing your duty is no offence by law. (20%)

5. **Tragedy of the Commons**

a. Grabbing the center grounds by the 'Powerful Elite' on the basis of inheritance, caste or some other criterion. And deprive the majority the fair distribution of the collective gains of progress. Especially applicable to extending hold over political power. (25%)

b. Casting rules and regulations under subterfuges to reserve many economic opportunities for groups and coteries and deny equal opportunity, e.g. reserves for small-scale sector, reserves for public sector units, etc. (25%)

c. Increasing the threshold for certain opportunities to deny general public or some targeted groups the equal opportunity, e.g. setting high qualifications to shut out entrepreneurs running startups. (20%)

d. Restrictive regulations in the name of regionalism, casteism or any other differentiation, e.g. 'son of soil', 'reserved for state residents only, etc. (20%)

e. Seeking to extend reservations for weaker sections beyond the limit mandated by constitution and law. (10%)

### B. Factors→Sub-Factors: Economy and Business

#### *Positive Factors*

1. **Economy Size and Growth**

a. A US$ 1.4 trillion economy, critical mass for a massive growth. (25%)

b. Growing at 7%+ rate despite global downturn. Good sustainability. (20%)

c. Solid fundamentals and all round strength (manufacturing as well as services). Long-term growth despite political inaction and logjams. (20%)

d. Institutional infrastructure for competitive economy. Financial, watchdogs, trade organizations active and effective. (15%)

e. Sufficient asset base, FE reserves and gold included. (20%)

2. **Immunity from Global Downturn**

a. Predominantly consumption based growth. (30%)

b. Distributed linkages. Well spread trade relationships. Less prone to sympathetic downturns due to economic meltdown in a particular region. (25%)

c. Competitive to hold on its own. (15%)

d. Not captive to any political alliance or military pact. Have the flexibility to realign or reconfigure trade or industrial partnerships. (15%)

e. Expanding portfolio of low priced new technology products. Can meet internal demands and help other nations boost their economy enablers. (15%)

3. **Private Sector Excellence**

a. Large and active private sector present in almost all sectors of economy. (30%)

b. Despite restrictions in certain industries (Defense and Telecom) earlier, the latent capabilities have come to the fore quickly to make up the lost opportunity, and has the capability to take on all large opportunities. (15%)

c. IT and BPO services excellence. (25%)

d. English language based skills a huge competitive advantage. (10%)

e. Collaborative processes with global leaders already in place and can be transcribed to other domains as well (high tech design and manufacturing and knowledge services). (20%)

4. **Development of Industrial Clusters**

a. Industries and their support entities forming clusters. This is increasing competitiveness and innovation in those industries. IT/Auto/Aviation clusters at Bangaluru, Chennai, Pune, Noida, Gurgaon and Hyderabad. Gujarat is developing a hub for auto industry. (30%)

b. Urbanization accelerating the process, e.g. new industrial clusters (Delhi-Mumbai corridor is one example) will provide impetus to process. (20%)

c. State governments competing for quicker industrialization. Opportunity for the new industries to choose the best environment (weather, availability of human resources, availability of enablers), location (closer to raw material sources, ports, etc.) and best governance (taxes, exemptions, etc.). (20%)

d. Certain areas of the country which are less developed, are likely to get due attention by the new technology industrial clusters, e.g. food processing and pharmaceuticals in Himachal Pradesh, tourism in Uttrakhand and other northern states close to Himalayas. (15%)

e. Transportation (road, rail, air, and shipping), and other enablers (power, water, etc.) likely to be developed keeping in view these clusters providing further boost to strengthening the synergy and innovation in these clusters. (15%)

5. **Diversified Economy**

a. Broad-based industry in all domains as any other advanced economy. (30%)

b. Both products and services industry. Advance services in IT, design and knowledge services. (25%)

c. All types of natural produce, agriculture, minerals, other raw materials available in abundance. Variety of whether conditions also assist specific type of conditions (temperature humidity, etc.) for specific type of industrial and agri-based industry. (20%)

d. Except energy (petroleum and uranium), no big dependence on outside world. (10%)

e. Abundant human resources for expansion of economy in a variety of combinations. (15%)

### *Negative Factors*

1. **Red Tape**

   a. Too much government in business. Right from making bread, telephones, shoes to major stuff-like airplanes. Not many government industries anywhere 'best in class' or even industry average. (15%)

   b. The obstructive policy framework that encourages reservations (monopolies and oligopolies) and inhibits entrepreneurship and competition. (25%)

   c. Interaction with various levels of governance machinery unpredictable and tardy. Discretionary powers to field officials are used to create encumbrances. (25%)

   d. Grievance handling system is a part of the same opaque governance machinery, with no assured response time. (25%)

   e. Plethora of regulations without relevance still exists on the rule book. Spittoons in offices, the relics of the past, still exist as a requirement, e.g. a number of inspectors, with no relation to any industrial activity still have the right and responsibility for ensuring fulfillment of conditions that no longer exist. (10%)

2. **Technology Dependency**

   a. Continued reliance on technology import. Strategic sectors like defense and aviation surprisingly suffer from these lacunae more than other domains. (30%)

   b. Even in private sector, technology development is more of an exception than the rule. No tax incentives for innovation. (20%)

   c. Policy heavily tilted in favor of 'one shot' asset induction rather than continuous engagement. More of trading rather than technology development needed for doing business with government. Private sector follows similar practices. (At least private sector is changing now). (20%)

d. Government R&D entities ineffective and waste of resources. In addition, they are blocking opportunities (by reserving high tech space for themselves) for private sector also. (20%)

e. Industry academia cross fertilization and synergic relationship almost absent. (10%)

**3. Lack of Excellence**

a. Lack of 'Best of the Breed' industrial units. (30%)

b. Heavy investment in socialistic pattern 'Public Sector' units (PSUs). The PSU hog much of tax payers' money (and industrial real-estate) and deliver pittance at productivity levels which are a fraction of global standards. (20%)

c. Corruption allows business entities to prosper without being best in class. Their survival depends more on negotiating the maze of contract capture rather than value delivery. So no motivation for being 'best of breed'. (20%)

d. Lack of fair competition. Too many qualification hurdles for the new and innovative startups or SMEs. (20%)

e. PSUs drag down the aggregate productivity at national level. (10%)

**4. Low Buyer Sophistication**

a. Government procurement is messy, opaque, slow and corruption ridden. (25%)

b. Private sector only slightly better. (15%)

c. Lack of level playing field. Qualification norms used to rule out most of the indigenous SMEs. (20%)

d. 'One shot' asset procurement is the norm. No procedures for development contracts or system lifetime engagement contracts. Asset value utilization poor. (20%)

e. System thinking missing. No systematic top down long-term operations or functional plan leading to a road map for a staggered procurement. Zero-based budgeting for each year is the norm. Asset base is an aggregation of ad hoc asset acquisition. (20%)

5. **Denial Regime**

a. Many high tech industries still reserved for PSUs. (30%)

b. Lack of competition has stymied technology development and no motivation for private sector to stick their neck out and innovate. (15%)

c. Steep qualification requirements are another form of denial regime. It forecloses opportunities for high tech organizations (including almost all SMEs) in India, while providing a 'easy to win' field to the 'military industrial complex' of the Western world and Russia. (20%)

d. Distress procurements at exorbitant spot prices and pressure to extract value from these expensive acquisitions create an infinite loop for import addiction and opportunity denial to the high tech innovators. (20%)

e. Defense and aviation are the evident cases, where indigenous industry has not been permitted to develop because of the mentioned strategy. This cycle is denying technology development in India while allowing foreign multinationals to survive even if they are faltering in their own markets (Westland, Bofors, Antonov and many others) at an exorbitant cost to India. (15%)

### C. Factors→Sub-Factors: People and Capability Development

***Positive Factors***

1. **Demographic Advantage**

a. Unique profile in the world, the ratio of workers to non-workers around 2:1 for the next 50 years. It is because India is a young nation with an age median at 26 years. India has larger percentage of population in work-age group than any other developing nation. (40%)

b. The fertility rate is just above replacement rate that means India is going to grow slowly leveling at a maximum population of 1.6 billion, so has a continuous growth of work age population till 2050, while the rest of the world has shrinking work-age group and Western world is depopulating. (20%)

c. The migration of work-age population from rural to urban areas is already underway and is likely to see half a billion more in industrial/urban centers. Most of this increase in urban population will be productive workers. (20%)

d. Even the non-workers will have a predominance of children, who are future workers. It is only after 2050 that India will start having increase in percentage of beyond work-age population. (10%)

e. Unique profile that will last till 2050. It comes at an epoch when rest of the industrialized world (Western and BRICS) has a shrinking work-age population. It is a monopoly advantage for the next 50 years. (10%)

2. **English Speaking**

a. Majority of the work-age population has working knowledge of English, the most efficient of industry language. (25%)

b. Hungry for educational excellence and professional progress, so English proficiency is widely sought. (25%)

c. Preference for engineering and medical disciplines long embedded in the psyche. These disciplines are almost 100% English medium. (20%)

d. A thread of continuity in English medium of instructions from primary, high and professional education. (15%)

e. Country wide colloquial acceptance of English language. (15%)

3. **Education and Training**

   a. Higher education institutions of world repute in engineering, information technology, management and medical disciplines. (30%)

   b. Predominance of agricultural background, so preference for salaried occupation. For the purpose education and training geared in that direction. (15%)

   c. Skill levels for industrial development available because of long tradition of working in collaborative projects in government and military sectors. (20%)

   d. Continuity training in corporate widely instituted. (15%)

   e. The education sector scaling quickly with participation of private sector. (20%)

4. **Preference for Engineering**

   a. Long established preference for engineering and medical skills. (25%)

   b. Indians rote learning and mathematical skills specially suited for design and software work. Success in California valley precedes Bangaluru. (20%)

   c. Success in IT and high tech has reinforced the preference for engineering. (20%)

   d. The engineering and management skills now becoming the requirement for the next stage of industrial development. (20%)

   e. The broad-based industrial growth spawning education, training and employment in new engineering disciplines, e.g. bio-engineering, aviation systems, etc. (15%)

5. **Lifestyle Enrichment**

   a. Heavy endowment of culture. Rich admixture of many cultures, religions and races of the world. Variety in life experience and cuisines. (30%)

b. Second largest entertainment industry in the world. (20%)

c. Historical monuments one of the largest treasures. Pleasure and education visiting some of the marvels of the earlier civilizations. (20%)

d. Variety of weather, from hot and humid to snowy mountains, rich tourism. (10%)

e. Secure and safe environment for social activities. (20%)

### Negative Factors

**1. Poor Primary Education**

a. Educational system still shows imprint of Thomas Babington Macaulay (Lord Macaulay's) policy for India under British rule, i.e. to create English literate workforce of clerks and minions. (15%)

b. Focus on rote and compliance and not related to challenges of the future. (25%)

c. Primary universal education infrastructure still remains poor, especially in rural areas. (20%)

d. Government investment is sub-optimal in primary education especially in rural sector. Private sector does not find it viable to invest in primary education. (25%)

e. Drop out rate one of the highest in the world because of social factors as well as bad implementation of education projects. (15%)

**2. Poor Budgetary Support for Education**

a. The political class still obsessed with control of minds rather than spawning/triggering independent thinking. Any revolutionary changes in education policy are not on the horizon. (25%)

b. Politicians' attention focused more on securing control of IITs, AIIMS and other institutions which are working well and should be given more autonomy. (25%)

c. No initiative/emphasis on expanding coverage of primary schools, which are the crucibles of our future. (15%)

d. Education budget allocation is a central government activity. Implementation has to pass through umpteen stages before reaching grass-root level, causing many leaks in implementation. (25%)

e. The governance machinery not geared up for any substantial uplift of the primary education system and is in fact a drain on the education outlays.(10%)

**3. No R&D Excellence**

a. Barring some exceptional individuals, Indians are generally missing from R&D award functions. It is not a preferred occupation. (20%)

b. Government has set up many institutions for research and development. Except space research and some defense systems (missiles), the institutions have not delivered the desired results. Instead, because of these institution, the research space is reserved for them and hence a closed option for private sector. (25%)

c. Corporate sector does not have an R&D outlook because of lack of opportunity in high tech sectors. Especially in high tech sector (defense, space, telecom, basic industries), there has been a long time restrictions. The thinking percolates down for other domains too, because it is more viable to be a trader than an innovator. This is finally changing with IT and pharmaceuticals. (20%)

d. Government themselves have no priority for R&D excellence. No tax breaks, no support for innovative startups, no space for new high tech organizations in government procurements. (20%)

e. Academic research and development is at low ebb. Hardly any synergy between industry and academia for many new concepts and systems, those routinely come out of colleges in the advance countries. (15%)

4. **Reservations Without Aim**
   a. Reservations are our Achilles heel. Rather than being tools of uplift and social equity, these have been misused more for perpetuation of entitlement. (30%)
   b. The (low income) sections that still need opportunities are not at the focus of current reservation disbursement. (20%)
   c. Reservations on omnibus basis are compromising certain core government functions and industrial efficiency. (20%)
   d. Reservations have been misconstrued by many as 'rights without prejudice', causing certain sections to depend on reservations rather than striving for excellence. (15%)
   e. Large percentage of reservation has effected the quality of education and in the long term, Indians are considered as only selectively employable by the Western world. (15%)
5. **Lack of Systems Thinking**
   a. "Jugaad", the method to get things done somehow, a millstone around our neck. This spawns tactical thinking in place of strategic planning and ad hoc measures in place of process driven approach. (25%)
   b. Long-term thinking, road maps, staggered plans are conspicuous by their absence. Emphasis is on yearly budgeting. Even our five year plans are aggregation of five yearly plans. That is why most of the aims are only partly fulfilled. (25%)
   c. The thinking in terms of life cycles or in respect of system evolution is conspicuous by its absence. Emphasis on repeating the action sequences of the past even if the scenario has changed. We have repeatedly imported technology for first, second,

third, fourth...generation of telecom, aviation, defense and heavy machinery, because we are thinking only in terms of yearly procurements. (20%)

d. Even at the highest level, the span of vision does not exceed till next elections. Even strategic pronouncements by any government may have validity only till the next elections. And the intervening time period may sadly be a couple of years only. (10%)

e. The cost of tactical thinking, in place of a judicious mix of strategy/tactics is exorbitant. We are not only buying second class assets and wasting financial assets, but also denying our own industry an opportunity to excel. (20%)

## D. Factors→Sub-Factors: Strategic Assets: Natural and Man-made Resources

### *Positive Factors*

**1. Abundant Natural Resources**

a. Endowed with immense natural resources. Fertile lands, water resources, temperate climate, forest wealth, mineral wealth and ample maritime assets. (30%)

b. Except energy (petroleum and nuclear fuels, but ample coal reserves), India can make do without much of imports of raw materials. (20%)

c. Water resources, though over-exploited in some regions lately, still have enough capacity for future growth. (20%)

d. Technology and systems for efficient usage of natural resources and renewable sources available. The solar and wind energy, though still largely unexploited, has conditions for a quantum increase in its harnessing. (20%)

e. Peninsula largely secure from cycle of disasters (despite coastal areas, and seismic zones alongside

Himalayas). Steady exploitation of natural endowment easy to plan and implement. (10%)

2. **Enablers for Industrial Development**
    a. Telecommunication, power, transportation, real estate development, civic services already in place. (20%)
    b. Policies and procedures in place, though not best in class. Competition between states accelerating the evolution of assistive policies. (25%)
    c. Education and training systems keeping up with human resources supply requirements of the industry. (15%)
    d. Clustering of various industries helping develop areas of excellence for various domains. Consolidation of upstream component industries helping efficiencies and sophistication of industries. (20%)
    e. The increasing sophistication inducing collaboration from MNCs to further accelerate the growth of industries. (20%)
3. **Financial System**
    a. A fairly developed financial system to support both corporate and individual needs. (30%)
    b. A balanced government and private sector banking system that allows both social sector focus and market focus. (15%)
    c. Automation (thanks to advanced software industry) at a high level of sophistication (even as compared to some Western nations). Can scale effortlessly to keep up with exponential growth. (25%)
    d. Extensive geographic coverage inside India as well as international. Can cater for expanding trade and supply chain relationships. (15%)
    e. Investment banks and foreign institutional investors actively engaged with industry. (15%)

4. **Educational and Research**

    a. Extensive primary education network (though requires a major overhaul). (20%)

    b. Higher education institutions of international repute. 'Best of class' institutions also setting up their campuses. (25%)

    c. Extensive research organizations (especially Bangaluru and Delhi area) in engineering and life sciences, agriculture and dairy (north India). Can provide a base for take-off for a larger effort. (20%)

    d. Academia research available and can provide an immediate expansion opportunity for industry. (15%)

    e. Extensive technical and industrial training establishments exist for working level skill development. (20%)

5. **Life Experience Improvement**

    a. Health services best in class, coverage low but scaling rapidly. (15%)

    b. Education expanse and quality scaling and improving. (20%)

    c. Entertainment. All media and contents expanding and qualitatively catching up with global standards. (25%)

    d. Information available openly, democratic openness (despite the recent government preference for selective censorship). (15%)

    e. Social life vibrant and invigorating. Cultural activities, festivals, sports and tourism flourishing. (25%)

### *Negative Factors*

1. **Unclear Division of Responsibilities**

    a. The resource development (real estate, industry, transportation, mines, financial infrastructure, education) a shared responsibility between various governing entities. The confusion sometimes results in both the governments shirking responsibilities. (25%)

b. The confusion creates an atmosphere where influence peddling and corruption takes charge. The scenario then changes to unbridled exploitation of 'common resources' for profit rather than common good. (20%)

c. The elaborate and lengthy allocations and permits are another invitation for influence peddling and corruption. Too many restrictions for real players and too much of leeway for the influential. (20%)

d. Political parties avoid mention of the growth-related responsibilities in their manifestos, which are filled with non-issues. This allows them to dereliction of their development responsibilities with impunity. (20%)

e. The bureaucracy is happy to be left with a lot of power without commensurate responsibilities in this confusion. There is no scrutiny of resource consumption v/s value created in the whole implementation machinery. (15%)

**2. Rehabilitation**

a. There is no long-term plan for the nation's re-organization in terms of landscape management. The urbanization, water resources re-organization (canals, dams, diversions), forestation, mineral resources development, etc. are planned piecemeal, so no one knows how the country is going to look like in 2020 or 2030, much less in 2050. (25%)

b. Displacement/migration of the people is a 'bolt from the blue', both for the displaced and even for the planners. In case of hydro projects, it has always been an afterthought. (25%)

c. The displaced people considered a problem rather than resources to be redeployed. They are generally not rehabilitated in a planned manner and remain a perpetually agitating block for their erstwhile homelands. (20%)

d. We are not able to develop areas that require manpower infusion, because we are wasting the displaced human resources for lack of strategy and plans. (15%)

e. The absence of an integrated approach (one ministry issues mining licenses and another carries the responsibility of rehabilitation and yet another responsibility of welfare of the tribal people) makes it impossible for the transformation of virgin areas to optimally leveraged natural resource assets. (15%)

3. **Bad Urban Infrastructure**

a. Bad inheritance. Overcrowded dilapidated cities and towns. (25%)

b. Low investment per capita, one sixth that of China and does not even compare with western standard. (25%)

c. Emphasis on problem alleviation rather than scaling. (20%)

d. Continuous uncontrolled migration to cities making things worse. (15%)

e. Low priority in government strategy. We are still making token commitments to urban renewal (a small-scale success) and almost no commitment to new cities (like China and Saudi Arabia). (15%)

4. **Low Investment**

a. Per capita investment lowest in industrialized world in urban infrastructure for current urban areas. (20%)

b. Two new cities Chandigarh and Gandhinagar in sixty years. China has created a hundred. (20%)

c. Policy paralysis in securing public private partnership for infra-development. (20%)

d. Centralized state control of urban governance. Not workable in a large country like ours. (25%)

e. No linkage between resources generated by a city and investment required for its expansion/upkeep. Resources diverted for political considerations. (15%)

5. **Process Paralysis**

   a. Emphasis on centralized control and exercise of absolute power rather than distributed efficient management processes. (20%)

   b. In absence of a top-down process definition, administration becomes aggregation of bottoms up actions. (20%)

   c. Emphasis on problem removal rather than capacity and quality upgrade. (20%)

   d. Process monitoring and enforcement totally absent. No scrutiny accepted in most of the government machinery (Lokpal bill notwithstanding). (20%)

   e. Real time course correction not a part of thought process. The authorities either exercise full discretion or are found to be facing the investigation of criminal conduct. Nothing in between. (20%)

## E. Factors→Sub-Factors: External and Internal Security

### *Positive Factors*

1. **An Established Military Force**

   a. A million strong well trained, experienced, dexterous, apolitical and patriotic military force. (20%)

   b. Additional 1.3. million para-military and similar numbers of police force. (20%)

   c. Extensive combat experience in country and globally. (20%)

   d. Apolitical, focused on defense. (20%)

   e. Extensive geographical presence. (20%)

2. **Infrastructure**

   a. Extensive infrastructure (real estate, transportation and communication) for military and paramilitary establishments, nation wide. (25%)

b. Established supply chain and industry linkages. (25%)

c. Support systems and organizations in place. (10%)

d. Integrated townships for separation from civil activities. (20%)

e. Special purpose organizations (storage, training, education, specialized medical system) in place. (20%)

**3. Structures, Processes and Systems**

a. Established organizational structures in place. Linkages with peer organizations and 'Command and Control' with political chain of command tried and tested. (25%)

b. Mature processes in place. Long established procedures and functions already established. (25%)

c. Operational systems in place. Though more conventional and need update to the evolving threat perception. (15%)

d. Linkages with government R&D and defense PSUs established. (15%)

e. Military diplomatic linkages also mature and working well. (20%)

**4. Operational Robustness**

a. Consistent 'Command and Control' between the civilian leadership and military/police executive. (25%)

b. Rich experience in various combat scenarios. (20%)

c. Leadership and force derived democratically from all sections of the society. Has cohesiveness and common commitment. (20%)

d. Pride and patriotism runs at a very high level (sadly, the same is missing in other sections of the India society), making their operational effectiveness a notch higher than other professional forces of the world. (20%)

e. Relocation allows the forces wider experience in adjusting to all geographical locations, be it snow bound areas, deserts, marshes or urban scenario. Great advantage for a ground force. (15%)

5. **Evolution of Technology**
   a. Dedicated defense R&D in government sector. (15%)
   b. Technology development in civilian sector at a high level and can be quickly adapted to defense use. (20%)
   c. Wide array of technology under deployment. Can be used as the base to evolve technology. (30%)
   d. Niche excellence can be developed for world class products and services. Satellite systems (thanks to space program) and radar systems (thanks to a coordinated effort by government R&D entities and private sector), and process automation systems (software predominant) can be our areas of excellence. (25%)
   e. We have a rich resource in academia research. Defense needs a direct linkage with this resource. (10%)

### *Negative Factors*

1. **Old Mindsets**
   a. Slow to evolve in keeping with the changing threat perception. (25%)
   b. Too much dependence on 'big bang' war doctrines of earlier times. (25%)
   c. Police not adequately focused on 'Law and Order' functions. (15%)
   d. The strategic political and services leadership still hesitant to prepare for the coming wars (internal and external low intensity warfare). (20%)
   e. Rigid organizational structures and entrenched classifications obstructing definition of required flat structures and new roles. (15%)

**2. Value Approach Missing**

a. 'Bang for the Buck' management approach missing. Huge investments are made but not monitored for value delivered. (25%)

b. Balancing of asset portfolio by monitoring utilization of defense assets and readjusting the mix not done. 'Security value per dollar spent' is not a favored practice. (20%)

c. No long-term efficacy/capability plans. Incremental budget hike YoY is considered the sufficient strategy. Big bang acquisition is generally a response to asymmetry threat rather than a part of capability maintenance. (20%)

d. No long-term association with anyone, a supplier, OEM or a integrator. India never gets the best price. Private sector ignored as a long-term supplier, and that is a huge commercial disadvantage. (15%)

e. Valuation of assets on book value and not on value delivery. This could be dangerous when India starts getting a larger global role. What then will matter is how we can handle new scenarios rather than how costly our equipment is. (20%)

**3. Asset Aggregation Mindset**

a. Asset aggregation approach abounds. Emphasis on numbers, force level, inventory and not efficacy. (More aircraft and tanks do not always make you militarily dominant, as Israelis have shown many times.) (25%)

b. No capability/functional road map (like the one published by US DoD), so no one (even in industry) knows which systems will be procured in future. This gives a disproportionate advantage to established MNCs, who can sell their last generation equipment, while it rules out innovative indigenous industry. (25%)

c. Technology base still patchy (state-of-the-art for aircraft, but poor in 'Command and Control' and support systems). We need to fill up all the sections of the pie. (20%)

d. We need to remove silos that our various arms operate in. Each arm wants to own exclusive assets (aircraft, UAVs, real-estate), rather than working out a joint usage paradigm. Consider that in the city of Mumbai, the commando team that went there to fight the terrorists could not get a bus for transport to the action site, despite so many organizations heavily involved in the operations. Duplication of assets is a colossal wastage in services. (15%)

e. Centralized asset acquisition is no more a viable strategy. Again, we are relating the acquisition to perceived requirement at ministry of defense rather than felt requirement at the operational level. (15%)

**4. Pro-Active Reorientation Missing**

a. Still hesitant to adopt new paradigms specifically for low intensity warfare. (30%)

b. The organization structure not evolving according to the changing scenario. For instance, homeland security is still not a potent anti-dote for terrorist attacks, and army being deployed for operations that are not in its line of specialization. (20%)

c. New systems like UAVs are still awaiting widespread adoption. (20%)

d. The thought process on matters triggered by 'Black Swan' events (Maoist attack, terrorists in Mumbai), and then goes to sleep again. No concerted effort to avoid the next attack. (15%)

e. Too much of political logjam in fashioning responses. National security paradigms cannot be subservient to political gamesmanship. (15%)

**5. Missing Synergic Coordination**

a. Various military and para-military (including police forces), still operate in silos. (25%)

b. The co-ordination (or absence of it) has been laid bare each time there is a terrorist attack. But sometimes the sovereignty and sometimes independence of the organizations is used to cover up the inability to be inter-operable. (25%)

c. The systems are not interoperable. The ad hoc acquisition does not permit the inter-operability schema to be a part of system design. (20%)
d. The inter-operability in 'Command and Control' schema is a desirable feature and not a commitment. The desirability generally gets put aside for convenience or idiosyncrasies of field commanders. (20%)
e. Value approach missing. So efficacy boost that inter-operability provides is not a matter of cardinal importance (as it should be). (10%)

## The Computation Schema

Now our information schema is complete. We will now devise methodology for constructing our Dashboard display for various data-sets in situations and times in India's road map to progress.

First we assign values to each of the 250 sub-factors that we have enumerated. We have come to a sufficient level of detail, so it is comparatively easy to estimate each of these values. We have chosen a scale of 1 to 5 for each of the sub-factors. Even if most factors are discontinuous values on fuzzy scale, e.g. (best, good, OK, below average, bad), we map them to (5, 4, 3, 2, 1).

The computation process proceeds as follows:

Assign values to sub-factors

⇩

Combine five related sub-factors to get each of the 50 factors
(25 positive and 25 negative)

⇩

Combine five related factors to get the positive and negative weights
for each of the strategy areas

⇩

Sum the positive and negative weights to get the Total Factor
Contribution for each of the strategy areas

The actual computations for Dashboard displays in this book were done on an excel sheet. The formulas used for computations are given below:

1. Sub-factors values: estimated for different epochs (2010, 2050 'Happy Scenario and 2050 Dismal Scenario').
2. Aggregation of sub-factors to factors

   Factor value = ΣSub-factor value × sub-factor weight.
3. Aggregation of sub-factors to factors

   Positive weight = Positive factor value × factor weight

   and

   Negative weight = Negative factor value × factor weight
4. Aggregation of factor weights to total factor contribution for a strategy area.

   TFC = Positive factor weight – Negative factor

## An Example Sub-Factor to Factor Computation on the Excel Sheet

A small portion of an active excel sheet (with assigned sub-factor values and calculated factor values) is pasted below for further elaboration of the flow of calculations.

As we can see, we aggregate the component sub-factors (multiplied with weights) to factor value, i.e.

Sub-factor 1 × weight 1 + ... + sub-factor 5 × weight 5 = Factor value

In the excel sheet we can see

5 × 30% + 2 × 15% + 4 × 20% + 4 × 25% + 5 × 10% = 4.1

What we can see is the summation of sub-factors of "Brand Equity" factor. There would be a similar computation for four other positive factors for this strategy area (Political and Regulatory Environment), and then for five negative factors.

| Area | Strategy Area | Factor serial | Factor | Sub-Factor Serial | Sub-factor | SF % Contri-bution | SF Value | Factor Value | Factor % Contri-bution | Factor Contri-bution |
|---|---|---|---|---|---|---|---|---|---|---|
| A | Political & Regulatory Environment | | | | | | | | | |
| | | 1 | Brand Equity | | | | | 4.2 | 20 | 0.84 |
| | | | | 1 | Stable Democracy | 30 | 5 | | | |
| | | | | 2 | Leadership Quality | 20 | 4 | | | |
| | | | | 3 | IT Excellence | 10 | 5 | | | |
| | | | | 4 | Quality of Talent | 25 | 4 | | | |
| | | | | 5 | Cultural Richness | 10 | 4 | | | |
| | | 2 | Enabling Policies | | | | | 4 | 20 | 0.8 |
| | | | | 1 | Clear Policy Enunciation | 20 | 4 | | | |
| | | | | 2 | Tranparent Interface | 40 | 4 | | | |
| | | | | 3 | Trade Promition | 10 | 4 | | | |
| | | | | 4 | Grievance Amelioration | 20 | 4 | | | |
| | | | | 5 | Participation Policy upgrade | 10 | 4 | | | |

### An Example Factor to Positive (and Negative) Factor Weights Computation on the Excel Sheet

A similar calculation of factors to positive factor weight (and negative factor weight) is shown below to elaborate the flow of calculations for (*Political and Regulatory Environment*), strategy area.

The computation schematic changes when we chose to increase the granularity to fourth level of detail, i.e. to micro-factors. For the purpose of discussions in this book, however, the third level of detail suffices.

| Strategy Area | Factor serial | Factor | Sub-Factor Serial | Sub-factor | SF % Contri-bution | SF Value | Factor Value | Factor % Contri-bution | Factor Contri-bution | Positive Negative Summation |
|---|---|---|---|---|---|---|---|---|---|---|
| Political & Regulatory Environment | | | | | | | | | | |
| | 1 | Brand Equity | | | | | 4.1 | 20 | 0.82 | 3.48 |
| | | | 1 | Stable Democracy | 30 | 5 | | | | |
| | | | 2 | Leadership Quality | 15 | 2 | | | | |
| | | | 3 | IT Excellence | 20 | 4 | | | | |
| | | | 4 | Quality of Talent | 25 | 4 | | | | |
| | | | 5 | Cultural Richness | 10 | 5 | | | | |
| | 2 | Enabling Policies | | | | | 3 | 20 | 0.6 | |
| | | | 1 | Clear Policy Enunciation | 20 | 3 | | | | |
| | | | 2 | Tranparent Interface | 40 | 3 | | | | |
| | | | 3 | Trade Promition | 10 | 3 | | | | |
| | | | 4 | Grievance Amelioration | 20 | 3 | | | | |
| | | | 5 | Participation Policy Upgrade | 10 | 3 | | | | |

# Bibliography


Barker, T., et al., "Technical Summary" in *Climate Change 2007: Mitigation. Contribution of Working Group III to the Fourth Assessment Report of the Intergovernmental Panel on Climate Change* [B. Metz, O. R. Davidson, P.R. Bosch, R. Dave, L.A. Meyer (eds)], Cambridge University Press, Cambridge, United Kingdom and New York, NY, USA.

"Beyond the BRICs: Updated Global Projections to 2050", *Economic Outlook*, PricewaterhouseCoopers, UK, March 2008.

Bhalla, Surjit, Ankur Chaudhary and Varun Khandelwal, "All You Wanted to Know (and more) about Inflation In India", *Developing Trends*, Vol. 1, Issue 1, March 2011.

Bloom, David E. (Harvard School of Public Health, Jan. 2011), "Population Dynamics in India and Implications for Economic Growth" in Chetan Ghate, *The Handbook of Indian Economy*, Oxford University Press, 2011.

Cycles of Civilizations: Memetic Reproduction, http://evolutionaryeconomics.wordpress.com/the-science-of-history/3rd-informative-age-metal-cycles/

Ferguson, Niall and Allen Lane, *The Ascent of Money: A Financial History of the World*, 2008.

Gandhi, M.K., *My Experiments with Truth*, Navajivan Publishing House, Ahmedabad (made available at www.apnaorg.com), Jan. 2012.

Gangulai, Sumit and Neil De Votta (eds.), *Understanding Contemporary India*, 2003.

Hill, K. et. al., *A Demographic Case Study of Forced Migration: The 1947 Partition of India*, 2003.

Holtz, Carsten A., *China Economic Growth 1978-2025: What We Know Today about China's Economic Growth Tomorrow*, November 2005.

Kosambi, D.D., *The Culture and Civilization of Ancient India in Historical Outline*, 1964.

Kwasnicki, Witold, *China, India and the Future of Global Economy*, 2011.

Lee, Jong-Wha and Kiseok Hong, *ADB Economics: Economics Growth in Asia: Determinants and Prospects*, No. 220, September 2010.

Madison, Angus, *Contours of the World Economy, 1-2030 A.D.: Essays in Macro-economic History*. Oxford University Press, p. 379.

Malmberg, Bo and Thomas Lindh, "Demographically-based Global Income Forecasts up to the Year 2050", Paper for Presentation at the Global Seminar on Age-Structural Transitions: Demographic Bonuses, but Emerging Challenges for Population and Sustainable Development, Organized by Committee for International Cupertino in National Research in Demography (CICRED), Paris, Republic France, 23-26 January 2004.

Mehta, Arun C., *Drop-Out Rate at Primary Level: A Note Based on DISE 2003-04 and 2004-05*, 2003.

Nehru, Jawaharlal, *Glimpses of World History*, The Johnday Company (made available at www.apnaorg.com) Jan./Feb. 2012.

Osterwalder, Alexander and Yves Pigneur, *Business Model Generation*, John Wiley and Sons, 2010.

*Oxford Economics: Can India Catch Up with China*?, September 2009.

Regions 2020: Demographic Challenges for European Regions, Directorate General for Regional Policy Brussels, November 2008.

Srinivasan, T., *China and India: Economic Performance, Competition and Co-operation: An Update*, 2004.

*Towards Freedom, The Autobiography of Jawaharlal Nehru*, Johnday Company, New York, Copyright 1941, Johnday Company.

Web Resources: The following websites are good sources of information related to the scope of this book. Many inferences drawn in this book, wherever possible, were substantiated against the generic trends described on many of these websites and other sources of information.

a. Project Syndicate: A World Of Ideas.
www.project-syndicate.org

b. World bank. www.worldbank.org

c. International Monetary Fund. www.imf.org

d. Asian Development Bank. www.adb.org/economics

e. Goldman Sachs Global Economics Website. www.gs.com

f. PricewaterhouseCoopers. www.pwc.com

g. Oxford Economics. www.oef.com

h. McKinsey Quarterly. www.mckinseyquarterly.com

i. Carnegie Endowment International Economics www.carnegieendowment.org

j. National Institute of Educational Planning and Administration. www.nuepa.org

k. The bank of Nova Scotia. www.scotiabank.com

l. Global Vision (Campaign for closer relationship between UK and EU). www.global-vision.net

m. Center for Strategic and International Studies www.csis.org

n. HSBC Global Research http://www.hsbcnet.com/gbm/about-us/global-research.html

o. Consortium for Research on Educational Access, Transitions and Equity
www.create-rpc.org

p. Planning Commission India www.planningcommission.nic.in
q. Indian Council of Social Science Research www.icssr.org
r. KPMG Infrastructure Practice www.kpmg.com/infrastructure
s. Indian School of Business. www.isb.edu
t. Organization for Economic Co-operation and Development. www.oecd.org
u. Commission on growth and Development www.growthcommission.org
v. Rand National Defense Research Institute www.rand.org
w. US International Trade Commission. www.usitc.gov
x. Memetic Cycles of Civilization http://evolutionaryeconomics.wordpress.com/the-science-of-history/3rd-informative-age-metal-cycles/
y. Brookings Institution. www.brookings.edu
z. Using World History to predict the future. www.worldhistorysite.com

Yeşilada, Birol, Brian Efird and Peter Noordijk, *Competition among the Giants, 2010-2050: US-EU-China and Implications for Regional Integration in Europe*, 2011.